THE TRUST IMPERATIVE

THE COMPETITIVE ADVANTAGE OF TRUST-BASED BUSINESS RELATIONSHIPS

Roger Dow, Lisa Napolitano & Mike Pusateri

The Trust Imperative

The Competitive Advantage of Trust-Based Business Relationships

Edited by:

Lisa Napolitano, Executive Director, NAMA
Sherry Kilgus, Director of Marketing, NAMA

Contributing Authors:

Doug Bosse, Senior Consultant, S4 Consulting;
Joseph Cannon, Ph.D., Asst. Prof. Marketing, Colorado State;
Mike Cohn, Manager Global Sales Programs, Hewlett-Packard;
Lance Dixon, Executive Director, JIT II Education & Research Center;
Patricia Doney, Ph.D., Assoc. Prof. Marketing, Florida Atlantic Univ.;
Roger Dow, Author *Turned On*, VP, Gen. Sales Mgr., Marriott Lodging;
Gerhard Gschwandtner, Publisher, *SellingPower* Magazine;
Jane Helsing, VP Strategic Accounts, QI International;
Sherry Kilgus, Director of Marketing, NAMA;
Gary Kunath, Principal, The Summit Group;
Jordan Lewis, Author of *The Connected Corporation*, and *Partnerships for Profit*;
Tom A. Muccio, VP, Cust. Bus. Dev. (Wal-Mart), Procter & Gamble;
Lisa Napolitano, Executive Director, NAMA;
John L. Neuman, VP, Integrated Supply Chains Segment, AT Kearney;
Dave Pearce, Supervisor Continuous Improvement Team, Chrysler;
Mike Pusateri, VP Interactive Sales & Marketing, Marriott;
Larry Smeltzer, Ph.D., Prof. Supply Chain Mgmt., Arizona State Univ.;
Joseph Sperry, Partner, S4 Consulting

For information about permission to reproduce selections from this book, write to:
Permissions, National Account Management Association
150 N. Wacker Drive, Suite 960, Chicago, IL 60606
Tel: 312-251-3131   Fax: 312-251-3132   Internet: www.nams.org

Library of Congress Cataloging-in-Publication Data

Napolitano, Lisa
        The Trust Imperative: The Competitive Advantage of Trust-Based Business Relationships / Lisa Napolitano, Mike Pusateri, Roger Dow

ISBN 0-9657422-1-0 $15.00

Printed in the United States of America.

Cover art by Harper & Case Ltd., New York, New York

Table of Contents

Part III: How-To

Part IV: Reference

FOREWORD

"They Must Be Crazy"

Jordan D. Lewis
Author of *The Connected Corporation*,
& *Partnerships for Profit*

FOREWARD

If UFOs turn out to be real and populated by intelligent beings, I suspect that one thing they would wonder about is why there is so little trust between many customer and supplier companies here on Earth. After all, any sensible visitor can see that we are economic and social creatures, that links between customers and suppliers are a central feature of our economies and that, when humans interact, trust produces better results. Because trust is scarce where reason would expect to find it, our visitors will conclude, "they must be crazy."

They may be right. Certainly the evidence suggests that trust between customers and suppliers produces superior performance. For example:

- A focus on trust between Ford and ABB was fundamental to their designing and building a car paint plant—an enormously complicated undertaking—in record time and at 25 percent less than the $300 million it would have cost in a traditional low-trust relationship.

- Thanks to a high degree of trust with all of its suppliers, Britain's Marks & Spencer has consistently been the most profitable general merchandise retailer in the world.

- Due to trust between Chrysler and its suppliers, this automaker enjoys the lowest per vehicle cost in its industry.

- For many years, Motorola and Philips Consumer Electronics have bought similar parts, materials and components, often from the same suppliers. While Philips uses conventional arms' length transactions to buy what it needs, Motorola depends on trust with its suppliers. Over the years, Motorola's purchasing costs have been dropping three times faster than those at Philips.

- Joined on the basis of trust, Butler Manufacturing, which makes and erects commercial buildings, and a major retailer cut the construction time for distribution centers from 180 days to 28.

If the results are so good with trust as the centerpiece of business relationships, why do we find so little? One reason may be customers' concerns about over-dependence on suppliers, although that can almost always be avoided. A second could be a mistaken belief that customers' use of power extracts the best results. Whatever the cause, discomfort between customers and suppliers has often endured for so long that reform to healthier relationships is defeated before it has a chance. Many companies say they want to change how they work with others until tradition calls a retreat. If we are to move beyond our current arrangements, we should first understand the barriers to be overcome.

A Troubled Past

Most companies, most of the time, are linked to others through arms' length transactions, which rely on definite terms such as price and specification to describe their relationships. By withholding all other data about its plans and processes, the supplier thinks it is guarding its margins; the customer believes it is avoiding reliance on the supplier, which might exploit this to win a higher price. The problem with this transaction mentality is that it encourages separateness.

With transactions, negotiations may be contentious because neither side has an interest in the other's well being. This promotes the art of deal making: what you get depends on cleverness and bargaining power alone. Information sharing is limited to what is needed to close the deal. Divulging more could yield an advantage to the other side. If, once you agree, an unexpected issue arises, you have little shared understanding and motivation to draw on to find a solution that works for both firms. Discomfort grows as unsettled or poorly resolved conflicts mount.

There is only so much you can do in transactions. These rigid, narrow ties inhibit joint value creation. With people's faith being in terms, rather than in each other, transactions spur finger pointing instead of joint problem solving. Simple scratches easily become festering wounds. This behavior is more appropriate to "Jurassic Park" than to competitive markets that keep demanding better results from everyone.

An Important Transition

To move from business as usual to cooperation, you have to overcome the habits that form with transactions. For some companies, this requires radical changes in mindset and style akin to converting a disagreeable opponent into a good friend.

Organizations are most effective together when they creatively join their ideas and energies. Such relationships thrive on information sharing and depend on each adjusting to the other's ways as they build together on new understandings. To do this, each firm's management, decision making, resources, structure, culture, politics and priorities must be aligned. While negotiations may sometimes be challenging, they are framed by an understanding that it is not in either firm's interest to hurt the other, thereby reducing its commitment.

Unlike transactions, where contracts spell out what you must do, no contract could describe the steps needed to blend the best from separate organizations or anticipate the creative responses needed to build together on new opportunities. While such relationships may include formal agreements, they depend primarily on trust.

A Promising Future

What are the chances that we will move toward trusting relationships? Until now, virtually the entire art of business thinking has focused on how a firm can wring more from its own assets. Many of the popular management tactics such as customer focus, downsizing and reengineering consider what companies can get done with resources they have on the inside. What customer firms have largely overlooked is that this orientation compromises a major opportunity for improving their performance.

Consider this. More than one-half of the average firm's revenues go to its suppliers. Dealing with those suppliers at arms' length gives a firm essentially what its rivals get. By contrast, working closely with suppliers to create unique value adds them to a firm's distinct competitive resources. In this light, the remarkable results I illustrated earlier are to be expected. This is a tremendous untapped potential for customers.

Trust-based cooperation between customers and suppliers thus seems inevitable—at least for customers that expect to survive in increasingly competitive markets.

PART I

THE FOUNDATION

CHAPTER I

An Idea is Born

Lisa Napolitano
Executive Director
National Account Management Association

Mike Pusateri
Vice President, Interactive Sales & Marketing
Marriott

CHAPTER I

The concept for this book came to life at the first Leadership Symposium sponsored by NAMA in the fall of 1996. There, academics and practitioners came together to discuss issues surrounding strategic account management. The symposium opened with a presentation by four academicians, two from the U.S. and two from Europe, who had scanned all the research and writing that had been done in the past 40 years on the subject of customer-supplier partnering. (This suggested reading list may be viewed and printed through NAMA's website, www.nams.org).

The academicians theorized that both research and study on the topic of national / global account management had gone through a series of cycles, with periods of little or no activity interspersed with spikes of high activity by both academia and the general business press. The presentation also noted that in recent years the area of national / global account management was being captured in a larger wave of academic research being done on *relationship management*.

The topic of **Trust** came out of a deliberate process to identify the core elements of successful relationship management practices. At this symposium, several of the academicians felt that **Trust** was the key component leading to critical factors in relationship management. During the meeting, the academics tested their hypothesis by dividing the practitioners in attendance into small groups to discuss the details of their most successful partnerships. They also discussed contributing factors to failed or struggling relationships. Upon close examination of the focus group feedback, it was clear that **Trust**, or lack thereof, was a frequent theme.

In the winter of 1997, NAMA launched a research study of its membership on the subject of trust in customer-supplier partnerships, the results of which are detailed in Chapter IX. Not only were the findings compelling, but the response of the practitioners to our attempt to better understand this elusive subject were favorable. And so, in the fall of 1997, NAMA set out to hold it's second Leadership Symposium with the objective of exploring the theory that *trust is central to relationship management*. The outcome of this landmark event is the collaborative effort that is *The Trust Imperative*.

Trust is something no amount of money and resources can buy; therefore it is a source of competitive advantage available to any party willing to adopt the appropriate mindset. It is dependent on the culture and values of organizations and the vast web of individual relationships that make up these living, breathing systems. When companies begin the collaborative process, they build critical linkages and networks between customer and supplier. They craft social / business contracts with teams based on partnership and empowerment principles. And at the highest level of organizational trust, the work teams take on a mutual vision, setting strategies and goals, and executing implementation under the guidance of a network of peer visionaries from both companies.

When both customer and supplier trust each other, they can share information and invest in understanding each other's business. Numerous studies cite **Trust**, or lack thereof, as <u>the</u> critical factor that distinguishes effective selling partnerships from ineffective ones. But characteristics such as trust, openness and honesty—which are slow to build and earn—are still not well understood.

At press time, new research profiled in the January-February 1998 issue of Harvard Business Review appears to have uncovered hard evidence that building trust really does pay off in bottom-line results. Professors from Wharton and Seoul National University studied the eight largest auto manufacturers in Japan, South Korea, and the United States, as well as 435 of their suppliers. Their results reveal that relationships with higher levels of trust had substantially lower costs. In fact, the automaker with the lowest trust levels spent nearly half of its face-to-face communications with suppliers on unproductive transaction-oriented matters, while the manufacturer with the highest trust rating had to use only a quarter of this time on such matters.

Researchers acknowledge that manufacturers that take an aggressive stance (re: non-trust-building) may secure lower component costs by pitting suppliers against one another. However, they are quick to point out that in markets where information is a valuable resource, the non-trust-building customer loses out on potentially valuable information from suppliers, who will save their knowledge for more deserving partners. Likewise, suppliers who do not have the trust of their customers are unlikely to be the recipient of customer-generated ideas about how they can improve their own operations. I would argue further that, as we approach the millennium, information is a valuable resource in *all* markets, and, thus, sources of information must be protected and nurtured as true assets of the corporation.

Alas, **Trust**, being largely invisible, is often overlooked. But what we have learned—what this book will show—is that **Trust** is a critical component in any strategic alliance.

CHAPTER II

What Is Trust?

Jane Helsing
Vice President Strategic Accounts
QI International

CHAPTER II

As it becomes evident that trust is a critical component of successful partnerships, it becomes useful to articulate exactly what trust is. At NAMA's September 1997 Leadership Symposium, three breakout groups of industry and university leaders brainstormed several aspects of this topic. This chapter reflects many of their conclusions.

In addition, QI International, a consulting firm which helps organizations enhance their key account relationship strategies, has developed an extensive database of quantitative and qualitative data on customers' requirements in numerous areas. The breakout groups' thoughts will be supplemented with research data drawn from this database.

What is Trust?

When asked to define trust, answers suggest two major components: actual performance and subjective feelings.

Starting with *actual performance*, trust in a supplier begins to develop out of a series of successful "deliveries," thus leading the customer to believe that the supplier is reliable when it comes to providing its products or services. Reliability encompasses quality of the deliverable, timeliness, appropriateness, and completeness. Reliability is often tracked in terms of operational measurements, and supplier management initiatives typically define those measurements at some point.

The second component, somewhat harder to measure, is that of *subjective feelings*. Reliability as defined above looks at previous performance, because solid past performance is perceived to be a better indicator of future success than sub-standard performance. But there is also a subjective element that is necessary to give customers confidence that, in fact, their needs will be met tomorrow.

In defining trust, the breakout groups often developed analogies. Thinking about marriage, partners ideally enter into this arrangement with a high degree of trust in each other. This trust developed out of more than simply "past performance." The trust that is felt is a special feeling, one that is reciprocal and participatory, and that involves interdependence of the two parties. It is a comfort zone. Those same words describe a trusting customer-supplier relationship. So how do the two parties get there?

Creators and Destroyers of Trust

In terms of performance, consistent performance over time is key to creating trust. Continuous improvement is also a necessary facet of this. In fact, customers are continuously raising standards for performance. Suppliers who do not demonstrate continuous improvement risk losing an opportunity to enhance the trust level of the relationship.

In describing the "soft" methods by which trust is either created or destroyed, the following behaviors were identified.

Open and honest communications. Whether outlining respective roles and responsibilities, developing common goals, or disclosing potential problems, open and honest communications provide fuel to the building of a trusting relationship. This is one of those areas that is often assumed (even overlooked) when it is present, but definitely missed when it is not.

Learning and accepting the other's value system. It seems as if trust develops more easily and quickly in some relationships than in others; when this happens, similar value systems are often implicitly acknowledged. For example, cultural similarities enable rapid understanding and acknowledgment of each other's value systems; where there are vast differences, it takes longer to determine whether or not compatibility in this area can be reached. Regardless of whether each other's value systems are the same, they must certainly be accepted. Likewise, a destroyer of trust is acting in a way that is knowingly contrary to the other's value system.

Maintaining confidentiality. In QI's research, input has been gathered from individuals in the customer role as to what contributes to a trusting relationship. A frequently mentioned theme was maintaining confidentiality. Customers often provide huge amounts of information to their suppliers, and regardless of legal confidentiality agreements, there must be a subjective level of trust. As one customer said to its supplier, "Many conversations probably cross the line, but I ... trust that what I share will remain confidential and only be used appropriately." When one thinks about what element of trust would be hardest to recover from after a fall, breach of confidentiality is probably in the running.

Walking in the other's shoes. This was voiced as being especially important for both the supplier and the customer. Whereas customers want to be assured that their interests are being cared for, the supplier also wants to be treated fairly. Another aspect of this discussed at the Leadership Symposium was the vulnerability in trusting relationships. Because of the knowledge that each party has of the other, there must be trust that those vulnerabilities won't be used to the other's advantage. In fact, a creator of trust is to help the other improve in its vulnerable area.

A destroyer of trust is greed. Greed represents disregard for what it is to walk in the other's shoes. It can be exhibited by either the supplier or the customer.

QI's research also confirmed these thoughts. Customers frequently mentioned that a trust-building behavior exhibited by their supplier was that the customer's needs were both understood and placed as a priority by their account team. Demonstrating commitment to the customer was described as a key element of a trusting relationship.

Traditions. Traditions form subtly over time. They contribute to the "special feeling" that is described in a trusting relationship. When major change occurs, either in an organization or in an individual relationship, it is sometimes the interruption to traditions that creates uncertainty in a once-trusting environment.

Can you evaluate trust?

In short, the answer is "yes." Although most organizations do not formally measure trust, there are both informal and formal approaches to its evaluation.

Informal evaluations. The Leadership Symposium brainstorming yielded the following ideas as to how trust is evaluated as being present.

- As an outsider, being accepted as an insider. For example, being issued your customer's company ID; being placed on their e-mail or voice-mail system.
- Expanding limits; i.e., being provided more latitude with fewer restrictions or "checks."

- Recognizing that the impact of failure is less damaging over time; in the most trusting relationships, the partners will help each other recover from a mishap.
- Seeing that the relationship has evolved to a new level.

Formal evaluations. QI's research has shown that you can also obtain a formal evaluation of trust from customers. This can be quantitative; e.g., "On a scale from 1 to 5, to what degree are we creating an environment of trust in our relationship?" More useful, however, is a question that requires a qualitative answer, as the responses are more actionable and beneficial.

The following reflects a composite of studies which QI implemented. Customers were asked to agree/disagree on a 5-point scale with the statement "XYZ fosters a relationship of trust with its customers." Those customers who responded with "strongly agree" supported their response with the following reasons. XYZ:
- Enables operational excellence for the customer
- Demonstrates commitment to the customer; e.g., with new products that help the customer's business
- Maintains long-term relationships
- Does what it says it will do

The customers who disagreed with the statement cited:
- Unresolved issues (e.g., pricing, legal)
- The supplier's financial (versus customer) orientation
- Concerns about product consistency

How much trust is required? It depends upon the importance of the relationship and the complexity of the interactions. Going back to the marriage analogy, more trust is demanded in that relationship than at the start of a dating relationship.

How does individual trust differ from organizational trust?

Organizational trust is generally more transferable; personnel changes can occur, and if the organizations are felt to trust each other, new personnel will likely assume similar attitudes. In individual relationships, trust must be proven and earned.

Organizational trust develops through reliable performance, as well as through consistent and supportive behaviors on the part of individuals. For individuals to impact organizational trust, they must have a high level of responsibility. Because organizations take on the characteristics of their leadership, it is important to recognize the role that the leader can have on organizational trust levels.

NAMs sometimes get caught in the middle of individual versus organizational trust. They constantly strive for trusting individual relationships, yet if internal resources don't deliver to the customer's satisfaction, a lack of organizational trust develops. This in turn diminishes the individual gains that had been made.

Summary

Trust is not an intangible over which individuals have no control. It should be communicated by senior management as a priority. It can be planned for and developed through both operational excellence and individual behaviors. Should it be lost, however, it is a difficult road to recovery, which is why maintaining trust is so important.

CHAPTER III

What Predisposes Buyers to Trust Suppliers?

Larry Smeltzer, Ph.D.
Professor of Supply Chain Management
Arizona State University

CHAPTER III

Most chapters in this book take the National Account Manager's perspective of trust. Little doubt exists, however, that trust is a two-way process. That is why words such as cooperation, communication and collaboration are used so frequently in conjunction with trust. Because trust is an interactive, two-way process, it is important to look at it from the buyer as well as the account manager/supplier perspective.

Because this chapter is written with the industrial buyer in mind, the terms common to this environment will be used: buyer and supplier. However, it is important to note that the same processes apply when considering National Account Managers.

The purpose of this chapter is to analyze trust from the professional buyer's perspective. The analysis will begin with a conceptual overview that will serve as a foundation for development of specific behaviors. The relative importance of these concepts will then be compared and discussed.

A Conceptual View of Trust

Many different definitions of trust can be provided and a wide variety is presented in this book. For practical purposes, however, most people simply know when trust exists or a high level of distrust prevails. And many managers believe this general feel is sufficient. To quote one manager, "It is like an aroma. We can't see it but we know when it exists and we certainly know a sour odor from a sweet aroma!" And another buyer said, "Trust is like a haze in the horizon...it is just there but we can't put our hands on it."

But a perfume salesperson must be able to distinguish among the many different types of aromas. If salespeople couldn't make distinctions among aromas, they wouldn't be capable of explaining differences and adapt to the changing needs of customers. The same is true for trust among buyers and sellers: the more that is understood about the differences, the more it is possible to adapt to different situations. And the more we know about trust, the easier it will be to create.

A Continuum

One way to conceptualize trust is to place the processes that create it on a continuum. On one end of the continuum is transactional trust. Transactional trust is created by economic forces. For instance, a buyer and supplier act in a particular fashion because to do otherwise would cost too much. An example is a supplier that delivers an order in a timely manner because a severe penalty is enforced if the delivery is late. The buyer can "trust" the supplier to deliver. On the positive side, trust results in a positive economic outcome. For instance, a buyer may trust a supplier and place a major order simply as a result of trust. This trust may reduce administrative costs associated with typical supplier evaluation procedures.

An easily recognized example of transactional trust is that we trust people to drive on the correct side of the highway. To break this convention means a heavy cost in a potential accident and a heavy fine. When driving along the highway, most people can be trusted to drive appropriately due to heavy economic sanctions. Transactional trust is so titled because it is determined by the economic transaction cost.

On the other end of the continuum are relational processes, which entail emotional involvement. The extreme instance of relational trust is when a spouse says, "I know he won't be late for the opera, he loves me too much!" Trust is built on emotions and relationships. Of course, buyers and suppliers don't love each other; however, they may not want to disappoint the other party. They may have a strong emotional involvement in each other's success. This end of the continuum is frequently referred to as the 'soft' end while the transactional processes are termed the 'hard' end.

An easily recognized example of relational trust is a supplier who assists a buyer with installing a complex piece of equipment. Although installment is not part of the purchase conditions, the supplier may want to assure that the buyer enjoys all the benefits of the equipment. It is important for the supplier to provide emotional support. Although the transactional outcome is important, relational process may supercede other considerations in this simple example.

The trust continuum is demonstrated in Figure 1. The important point to note is that different amounts of these two types of trust may exist in any particular situation.

T r u s t   C o n t i n u u m

T r a n s a c t i o n a l T r u s t	R e l a t i o n a l T r u s t
e c o n o m i c c o s t s / b e n e f i t s	e m o t i o n a l i n v o l v e m e n t

FIGURE 1

Cognitive Processes

Another conceptual model of trust is based on the cognitive processes used to develop trust. This model is also presented in the chapter within this book written by Cannon, Pusateri and Doney. According to this model, trust can occur as a result of one or a combination of five different processes:

- calculative process
- prediction process
- intentionality process
- capability process
- transference process

As you read about these processes, keep in mind that they may be rather intuitive. In other words, people don't systematically and logically analyze the extent to which they trust. Also, while these five processes are described and discussed separately, they are actually overlapping, integrated processes. They all operate concurrently but to different extents.

The *calculative process* is similar to transactional trust in that it is based on the economic cost/benefit of a behavior. In this process, the buyer simply calculates what it would cost a supplier not to meet some relationship condition. If the buyer concludes that the supplier believes an untrustworthy behavior to be too costly, the buyer trusts the supplier.

One side of the calculative process is based on fear: How much does the supplier fear not being trustworthy? The buyer can increase trust by adding penalties to the supplier to act otherwise. For instance, any slight performance deviation may result in a payment penalty. Or, any cost misrepresentation in a partnership later detected by the buyer results in a penalty.

The *predictive process* is based on the buyer's ability to forecast the supplier's actions. Trust is based on past history. The buyer's assumption is that the supplier's past performance will be an indicator of future behavior. The buyer is essentially saying, "Based on past performance, I can trust the supplier."

When the buyer and supplier have done extensive work together, it is easier to use the predictive process. Also, the broader the range of past experiences, the greater the tendency to use the predictive process. This range of experiences could expand to social interactions, which provide an argument for activities that expand beyond the normal work environment.

Trust is based on the *intentionality process* when motives are evaluated. If the buyer believes the supplier has the best intentions, trust will result. This process is similar to relational trust discussed earlier. This process requires a psychological interpretation that may be based on persuasive tactics.

When considering intentionality, the question is what persuasive strategies convince the buyer that the supplier has the best intentions. The buyer wants to know that the supplier will not try to take advantage of any situation. In other words, the buyer must be persuaded that the supplier is not an opportunist.

The *capability process* is used to determine if the supplier has the ability to meet its obligation. Compared to the other processes, all that is asked here is "can the supplier do what it says it can do?" Objective capabilities are the concern, rather than abstract cost/benefit analysis, past performance, or intentions.

The contemporary buying professional is often said to be only a "spread-sheet analyst." This means that the buyer only analyzes the objective criteria. This is trust based on the capability process. If all the analytical tools indicate that the supplier will perform, then the buyer believes that the supplier can be trusted.

The final cognitive process used to establish trust is the *transference process*. Similar to intentionality, this is a social psychological process. "Company X has always been trustworthy; therefore, salesperson Y who works for X must be trustworthy." This is the transference process in action. It is the cognitive process that transfers the buyer's trust of an individual, organization, or institution to a related party or entity. Conversely, distrust may also be transferred.

One example of transference may apply to a new, inexperienced account manager. The buyer may have no experience with this account manager, not know the individual's capability or have any understanding of the account manager's intentions. However, the buyer has extensive trust in the account manager's organization. Or the transfer may occur in the other direction—trust in an individual transfers to an organization.

In summary, two models for conceptualizing trust have been presented. One model considers trust along a continuum and the other model presents five different cognitive processes. But the question exists: what is the predominant manner in which buyers develop trust? Furthermore, what implications does the trust development process have for buyer-supplier relationships and negotiations?

Buyers' Comparison of the Processes

In order to provide an in-depth answer to these two questions, semi-structured interviews were conducted with 26 professional buyers. Although this is a limited number of buyers, the results provide valuable insights about what predisposes buyers to trust suppliers.

The interviews began by explaining the conceptual perspective on trust similar to the discussions provided in this chapter. First, the nature of relational and transactional trust was presented. A diagram showing the continuum in Figure 2 was presented to each interviewee.

Extent to Which This Process is Used to Develop Trust					
Transactional Processes			**Relational Processes**		
3	**2**	**1**	**1**	**2**	**3**
High		**Low**	**Low**		**High**

FIGURE 2

The interviewees were asked to allocate 100 points to the six positions on the diagram. The 100-point allocation was to indicate the extent to which either transactional or relational concepts were used to develop trust in suppliers. The results are presented in Table 1.

TABLE 1 Buyers' Weight Placed on Relational and Transactional Processes						
	Transactional Processes			**Relational Processes**		
Value	3	2	1	1	2	3
	High		Low	Low		High
Cumulative Weight	600	430	470	490	320	220

The conclusion is clear and rather dramatic: much less emphasis is placed on relational processes than transactional processes from the buyers' perspective.

What does this mean from the NAM's perspective? The economic factors develop a much greater trust that the desired results will occur than the relational, emotional processes.

The next part of the interview explained the five cognitive processes detailed in this chapter. After the five processes were explained, the buyers were asked to rank order the processes' importance in developing trust in suppliers. The rank orders of the 26 buyers were then accumulated, and the average rank orders are presented in Table 2.

TABLE 2
Average Rank Order of Five Trust Processes

Process	Average Rank Order
Capability	1.63
Predictive	2.30
Calculative	2.77
Intentional	4.07
Transference	4.23

Again, the conclusions are clear and rather dramatic. First, capability is the strongest process leading to trust. The buyers are simply saying that if the suppliers have the capability to perform, they trust that they will perform. The highest ranked process takes on additional credence when considered with the second most highly ranked process: predictive. These two processes in combination indicate the importance of a trust development process that is objective. It is clear that the buyers allow performance to lead to trust.

The two more subjective or social psychological processes, intentional and transference, are significantly less important in the trust development processes. It seems that neither trust through association nor trust via good intent are as powerful as the actual capability to perform.

Both the capability and predictive processes are highly related to actual performance. The third highest ranked process, calculative, is not directly related to performance; however, it implies that performance can be trusted to occur because of objective economic conditions.

Meanwhile, the social-psychological processes of intention and transfer were given significantly less emphasis by the buyers. The conclusion can be made that the interpersonal, psychological processes tend to have less effect on trust than the objective, quantifiable processes.

An important relationship exists between the two conceptual models discussed with the professional buyers. On the continuum from transactional to relational, much more emphasis was placed on the transactional end than on the relational end. The points were allocated on a greater than 1.5 to 1 ratio to the two ends of the continuum. The transactional end may be considered more objective or "hard" as it involves a cost-benefit analysis. Meanwhile, the cognitive processes that were most emphasized are the more quantifiable or "hard" processes. In both models, the relational or soft processes received less emphasis.

Implications and Recommendations

How can this information about trust process help develop more effective buyer-supplier relationships? Although the information was obtained from buyers, the following discussion is directed toward the supplier or account manager side of the equation.

The first implication from the prior discussion and findings from the interviews is that data is important. The buyers seem to base trust on suppliers as a result of their capabilities. This is only logical. But comments from the buyers when discussing capabilities provide further insights. For instance, when one buyer was talking about a service supplier, she said, "Everyone tells us that quality is important. They can give me all kinds of stories about quality. But what really talks to me is data."

The significance of this quote is enhanced by related comments made by this buyer. She emphasized that results meant performance on other projects completed by the supplier. On several occasions she used the phrase, "Put facts in my face. Once I see the facts, I will trust them." These comments seem to de-emphasize the impact of a sales presentation that does not emphasize capabilities supported by facts. In 16 of the 26 interviews, the buyers mentioned the importance of facts when developing trust of suppliers. No doubt this group of professionals want objective, quantifiable information.

Highly related to capability is the predictive process. It may be relatively easy to establish trust if a good working relationship has been developed. But the interviews indicate that the relationship can be enhanced by providing performance data that indicates past and current capabilities. In other words, quantified past performance enables buyers to predict trust in a future transaction. Based on these findings, a recommendation is to develop trust by documenting capabilities with quantifiable information.

A related recommendation is for supplier representatives or NAMs to have an in-depth understanding of the product or service they represent. A major complaint of the buyers was that product or service knowledge was lacking. To quote one buyer, "It is difficult to have trust when I am not sure they even understand their product." Similar comments were presented in 18 of the interviews. This conclusion from the interviews is supported by other research of purchasing professionals. To implement this recommendation, it is important to conduct extensive product training in addition to training on sales techniques.

The opposite side of these recommendations relates to what should be avoided. First, it is important not to rely on good intentions. A supplier can show good intentions by providing expert testimony. Or good intentions may be indicated by follow up sales calls and general enthusiasm. Some NAMs may believe that extensive social contact may indicate good intentions that translate to trust. The evidence presented here does not support this belief. However, it is important to note that efforts to display good intentions could be combined with demonstrations of capabilities. As one buyer stated, "I don't mind follow-up or strictly social calls, but I really want to know what the product can do for me."

Transference is another process that had much less impact on trust than capability. This is important because the buyers were clear that just because one corporate division demonstrated capability trust did not necessarily mean that it transferred to another division. In fact, trust in one product does not necessarily seem to transfer to another product within the same company.

The lack of transference can be generalized to company representatives. The general conclusion drawn from the buyers was that each person had to develop their own trust from the buyers. The recommendation is that NAMs should not put much confidence in their ability to obtain trust from buyers as a result of the company's or colleagues' positive reputation.

In this discussion, relative importance of trust processes have been reviewed, concluding that capability and calculative (transactional) processes have the greatest influence on trust. However, it is important to remember that the various processes can be combined in order to generate trust. Also, it would be inappropriate to conclude that the lower ranked processes do not have the ability to generate trust—each situation may be different.

Summary
Trust may be an easy concept to discuss, but it is difficult to understand. The relative importance of different trust processes leads to some initial understanding of how professional buyers develop trust of suppliers. In-depth interviews of twenty-six buyers indicate that transactional processes have more effect on trust than relational process. In addition, capability, predictive and calculative processes have more affect than intentional and transference processes.

As a result of the interviews, five recommendations are presented. First, develop trust by documenting capabilities with quantifiable information. Second, emphasize the value of past performance with the supplier by documenting quantifiable results. Third, have an in-depth of understanding of the product and services in order to fully explain the capabilities. Fourth, do not put extensive emphasis on developing messages that simply promote good intentions. Capabilities must be presented in addition to the good intentions. Finally, limited trust can be expected to transfer from one person or product to another one within a company.

CHAPTER IV:

Trust in Strategic Relationships: A Requirement?

John L. Neuman
Vice President Supply Chain Management Practice
A.T. Kearney, Inc.

CHAPTER IV

If you asked a group of people how important trust is to business relationships between companies, you would probably expect them to answer 'very important.' And I concur - trust is an important part of an advanced relationship. But looking deeper into advanced relationships and the context in which trust plays a role can lead to some interesting discoveries. One of these discoveries is that, in and of itself, trust is not a suitable objective of an advanced relationship. Trust must be understood within the context of a company's overall business strategies and how relationships of all kinds are intended to support these strategies. Depending on the strategy, the role and importance of trust can be overestimated, underestimated, or misunderstood.

The Meaning of Trust
A quote by N. Kumar said:

> "Trust is stronger than fear. Partners
> that trust each other generate greater
> profits, serve customers better, and are
> more adaptable."*

I believe most people would embrace this idea and view this as how trust is leveraged in business. However, as powerful as this statement is in its simplicity, I believe it requires thoughtful dissection.

Kumar talks about "partners that trust each other." Simply trusting each other is insufficient, at times even danger-

---

* Harvard Business Review November/December 1996

ous. Trust has to be earned first, and then sustained, by both sides. Within this context, an organization that does not perform consistently well *all* the time is not worthy of trust, no matter what "relationship" it has with another organization.

The second portion of this quote portrays the payouts for trust—greater profits, improved customer service and adaptability. While these are possible by-products of trust, this statement brings up some interesting questions: How does trust link to these payouts, and under what conditions? What is the connection between trust and growing a business, compared to taking cost out of the business through better inventory control or providing better customer service through streamlining? And, in the context of relationship-based strategies, in what direction have leading companies moved, and what other variables besides trust generate improved profits and market share?

Voices of Advanced Relationships

The concept of trust typically conjures up words such as predictability, fairness, honesty, confidentiality, openness, candor, empathy, disclosure and belief. While these words do not mean exactly the same thing, they illustrate some of the different behavior and relationship possibilities that might be incorporated into relationships that are intended to support a business strategy.

Throughout this chapter, I will be referring to a particular market-based research study* sponsored by eight companies—IBM, Packaging Corporation of America, Pope and

---

* This Consortium Benchmark Survey was originally conducted by Meritus/IBM updates in 1997 by A. T. Kearney

Talbott, Dominick's, Monsanto, Whirlpool, Kodak, and Snow Brand—in order to probe deeply into advanced relationships among enterprises in those supply chains that flow physical goods through to retail outlets and ultimately, consumers. As part of this research, more than 200 companies were interviewed in depth from five different supply chain segments: raw material and package suppliers, finished goods manufacturers, third-party logistics and transportation companies, distributors, and retailers.

One of the international manufacturers in this study—a leader in the United States—said that "what trust boils down to, in a nutshell, is credibility." Another manufacturer, one of the best in the world, talked about confidentiality and the fear that in the old days sales people would tell one account what another was doing. This issue of holding a confidence is an important concern and risk as organizations become more open. For example, suppliers will learn things about their retail customers that must not migrate to the retailer's competitors.

A retailer in the study talked about openness and the sharing of information that traditionally is not shared unless there is a long-term relationship and a sense of trust. A leading consumer goods company also spoke about openness and the effect it had on a relationship. As soon as the company started sharing its most confidential strategic plans with a particular retailer, the two companies' relationship transcended to a new level. They were able to get things done faster and solve problems much more easily based on this simple but highly confidential sharing of information.

The challenging question then is how do these various aspects of trust get built into high-level alliances and produce numerous types of objective payouts in shareholder value, customer satisfaction, share growth, and profits?

Trust and Advanced Relationships

Without a doubt, trust is one of many components of advanced relationships (see Figure 1). In turn, advanced relationships are needed to have advanced practices and leading-edge core capabilities. And it is advanced practices that then lead to outstanding performance.

Putting trust into context

Figure 1

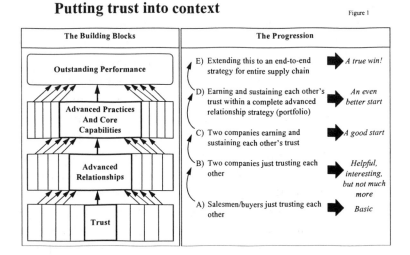

For example, trust and advanced relationships can lead to advanced practices such as vendor-managed inventory, which can lead to better inventory turns and greatly increased speed to market. In this study the benefit of truly advanced relationships cited most by the 200 companies was revenue growth (see Figure 2). The second most cited benefit was lower costs.

The challenge overall is how to create and extend trust throughout the entire supply chain (end-to-end), creating advanced relationships that then lead to advanced practices and finally, desired payouts. Most of the advanced practices in use or being contemplated today require new, multi-enterprise alliances or partnerships throughout the entire supply chain. Companies that are unable to enter into and sustain these advanced, supply chain relationships will fall to the wayside, and those that can will become the category dominators in profits, growth, share and customer/consumer satisfaction.

Increased sales was number one benefit

Figure 2

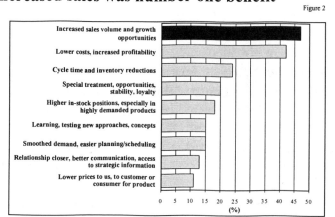

Source: Consortium Benchmark Survey

To illustrate how this works, let's take a look at the cycle time for manufacturing carpets through to home installation. A few years ago carpet production, measured from making the fiber through to installation of the carpet, typically took 16 weeks for its supply chain.* One leading fiber company envisioned a process that, through advanced relationships and the coordination of multiple enterprises,

---

* Business Process Reengineering: BreakPoint Strategies for Market Dominance, Henry J. Johannsson, Patrick McHugh, A. John Pendlebury, William Wheeler III, John Wiley & Sons, 1993

might be reduced to only one week. Within one week from the time a person walked into the retail space and placed an order, the fiber would be cut, died, tufted, etc., and the following weekend the customer would have the carpeting in the home. This leading company's advanced supply chain has made significant progress toward this one-week goal through fundamentally different and advanced enterprise relationships with new forms of trust at work.

Supply Chain Excellence

Advanced supply chain excellence requires companies to move outside their own functional silos, beyond just cross-functional improvements within their own enterprises and past new linkages with their most immediate suppliers/vendors and customers. The necessity is to create totally linked supply chains (end-to-end) that allow their participants to compete not just as individual enterprises, but as complete supply chains.

To make this jump successfully, there are five key flows that must be uniquely and effectively integrated for the greatest payouts to be achieved (see Figure 3). These flows no longer work in merely a linear way, but as an interdependent and enabling network of products, electronic funds, open information, value-added services and advanced relationships.

Five key flows are critical

Figure 3

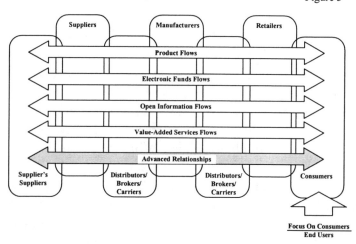

Putting Trust Into a Strategic / Operational Relationship Context

As part of this research, the 200 participating companies provided insights into:

- Supply chain inefficiencies and initiatives
- Their expectations of their suppliers and customers, and what they believed were the expectations of their suppliers and customers in return
- Examples of especially effective, innovative and highly productive relationships.
- History, structure, and workings of these relationships
- The relationship strategy and culture within their own organizations
- A visioning exercise as to what would constitute the perfect supply chain

Senior-level executives were asked to tell their companies' stories. This study did not consist of a written survey with short answers and check-offs, as most large-scale research is conducted. Rather, probing but non-leading questions were used that avoided using words such as "partnership" or "trust." In essence, the executives were asked to talk about and explain, in depth, examples of highly effective and/or innovative relationships. How did they come about? What's particularly good about them? How are problems solved within the relationships? What are the payouts and how did they know?

The answers were tape recorded and transcribed so that the language actually used could be manipulated as to what was said, how it was said, and the context within which it was said. Cutting-edge language-context analysis* was then used to determine what exactly the participants were saying and how it related to everything else they were saying. For example, if they used the word "trust," it was known whether they were referring to "openness," to "credibility," or to some other element of trust. Through language-context analysis, all described relationships were mapped and segmented as to win-lose characteristics, buying behaviors and many other variables and attributes. One of the advantages of this cutting-edge technique is that at any time one can go back to the material and, using the same context in which every important thing was said and how it was said, conduct additional analyses on emerging issues, thus producing new insights even years later.

---

* Using techniques/tools developed by the Center for Strategy Research (CSR)

Research Findings

Among the voluminous findings of this extensive study are ten of some note that provide the fundamental building blocks for advanced practices based upon advanced relationships, and that illuminate the correct role of trust.

1. New Model Emerging

The New Model for supply chain management relies on highly cooperative relationships among the members of a supply chain (see Figure 4). The emphasis has moved from a company being driven to serve its immediate customers to the idea that the entire supply chain should focus all the way down the chain to the ultimate buyers or consumers. If an upstream supply chain member two or three enterprises removed from the consumer does not know what is happening at the consumer end, the supply chain will remain stuck in the old model and will not keep up with what the most advanced players are doing today and working on for tomorrow.

There is a shift to highly advanced relationships and new practices
Figure 4

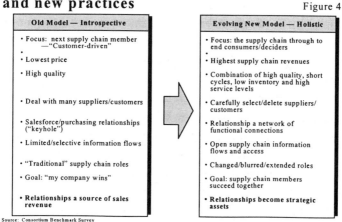

Old Model — Introspective	Evolving New Model — Holistic
• Focus: next supply chain member —"Customer-driven"	• Focus: the supply chain through to end consumers/deciders
• Lowest price	• Highest supply chain revenues
• High quality	• Combination of high quality, short cycles, low inventory and high service levels
• Deal with many suppliers/customers	• Carefully select/delete suppliers/ customers
• Salesforce/purchasing relationships ("keyhole")	• Relationship a network of functional connections
• Limited/selective information flows	• Open supply chain information flows and access
• "Traditional" supply chain roles	• Changed/blurred/extended roles
• Goal: "my company wins"	• Goal: supply chain members succeed together
• Relationships a source of sales revenue	• Relationships become strategic assets

Source: Consortium Benchmark Survey

One very large agra-based supplier of raw ingredients to food manufacturers is moving toward the New Model, trying to learn more about its key customers' *customers*. By striving to ensure that they and all of their upstream and downstream partners fully understand the demand and operational characteristics of the entire supply chain, this company hopes to unleash the power of the chain and generate the highest supply chain success.

Open flows of supply chain information are part of this New Model. In recent years, the Internet has been an important and growing enabler facilitating this access. The New Model also includes new dynamics of deleting both suppliers and customers that will not fit in smoothly into the five key flows shown in Figure 3. In the study there were many examples of major companies that have cut customers off that would not or could not adjust to the new way of doing business. The relationships had become just too much trouble and thus unworkable for the new advanced practices being deployed (e.g., VMI, cross-docking, co-forecasting).

The New Model also contains relationships that are evolving into a complex network of inter-connections among enterprises. No longer are the relationships maintained by just two key people—typically a buyer and a seller. The New Model calls for multiple contacts to take place at several functional levels. A well-known example of this is the Procter & Gamble-Wal-Mart relationship. P&G has a substantial, full-time team working with Wal-Mart in Bentonville, Arkansas, which allows P&G to interact with Wal-Mart at several functional levels (e.g., IT-to-IT, finance-to-finance, store ops-to-store ops, and so forth). The key to this evolving New Model is to make relationships strategic assets that are invested in, and that appreciate in value for all parties through demonstrable improvements in revenues, costs, assets and, ultimately, shareholder value. Figure 5 shows the differences in shareholder value creation (SVC) as it relates to success in advanced relationships.

Advanced relationships do pay out

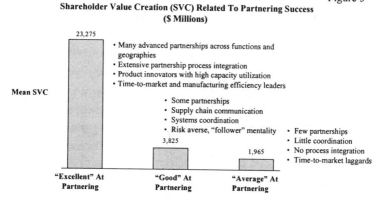

Figure 5

Shareholder Value Creation (SVC) Related To Partnering Success
($ Millions)

Source: 1997 A.T. Kearney High Tech Value Survey of 76 high-tech companies studied by industry segment

2. Performance Before Performance

Companies have to earn trust through their unswerving performance. As the complete highly linked and interdependent supply chain becomes more important, companies will not maintain relationships with an enterprise that cannot perform well within the supply chain. Performance problems deteriorate trust at every step until a customer or supplier begins to look elsewhere to find a better relationship.

3. Closing the Expectations Gap

During the survey, we had retailers and manufacturers talk about what they expected and what they believed their counterparts would say they expected in return. Figure 6 shows what manufacturers believed their retailers would say and what those retailers actually did say. Remember that no leading questions or prompts were used—everything was based on unaided recall.

Retailer's expectations of manufacturers

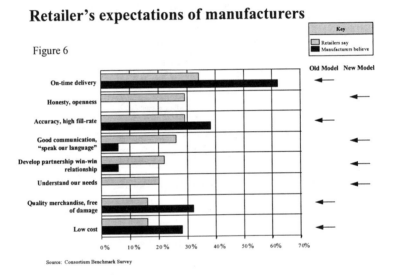

Figure 6

Source: Consortium Benchmark Survey

Retailers want honesty and openness from their manufacturing vendors; they want their needs to be understood; they want good communication and manufacturers that "speak their language"; and they want win-win partnerships. These variables are associated with the New Model, and, by and large, manufacturers did not know retailers expected these things. In regards to their retailers, manufacturers are still thinking in the Old Model way—low cost, damage-free, on-time, and so on.

This pattern continued, only in reverse, when we compared what manufacturers want to what retailers think they want (see Figure 7). By and large, the greatest mismatches occurred in the softer, New Model variables. The manufacturers say win-win relationships are very important, while retailers don't see these as a manufacturing interest. The same goes for good communications. What this means is that while both sides believe that the softer side variables - openness, partnership, honesty, trust - are very important to them, they don't perceive that they are important to the other side.

Manufacturer's expectations of retailers

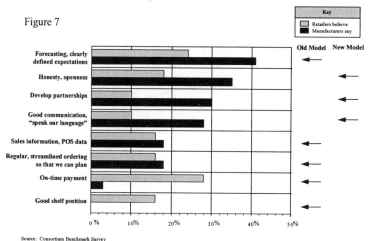

Figure 7

Source: Consortium Benchmark Survey

Most corporations believe it takes time to develop truly advanced relationships and install advanced practices. The typical estimate is three to four years. However, the data showing that all parties rank softer side, New Model variables high indicate that a much more rapid path of migration to better supply chain practices is possible because the other side is more likely to be willing to make these moves than previously thought.

4. Relationships as a Portfolio
From the descriptions of outstanding relationships, it was determined through statistical analysis whether statistically significant and different types of relationships were being described. In fact, there were four different kinds of highly successful and advanced relationships, which are shown in Figure 8.

Highly Successful And Advanced Relationships

Figure 8

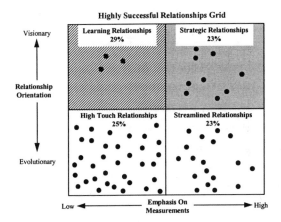

Highly Successful Relationships Grid

Source: Consortium Benchmark Survey

The x-axis in the figure shows the degree of emphasis the company places on measurements. When the executives spoke about relationships that fell into the two right-side quadrants, they talked about measures and accomplishments. Things like lower costs, higher inventory turns and higher service levels came up often. Executives that discussed relationships that fell in the two left-side quadrants basically didn't talk about measurements at all. This doesn't mean that the companies involved in these relationships did not measure anything. On the contrary, these are sophisticated companies that measure quite extensively. However, with these relationships, there were many more important characteristics than what was being measured. The y-axis measures the "orientation" of the relationship. Orientation in this case means whether the relationship evolved or if it was more proactively developed and more visionary in nature.

Legacy or evolutionary relationships fell into the lower two quadrants. In the lower left, High Touch quadrant, are examples of relationships that have evolved to a given state without extra investment or much change going on in the relationship. High Touch relationships exist in the comfort zone. If things go wrong, the parties make it right. They go the extra mile and take care of each other. However, things do go wrong with business processes in this quadrant because the processes have not been fundamentally upgraded. Every now and then a late shipment occurs or an order is dropped. When this happens, they cover for each other. High Touch relationships are considered very successful by those companies that described them.

The Learning relationships, upper left quadrant, were proactively sought, and significant management time and resources have been invested. The Learning relationships are experimenting and creating prototypes. While measuring was taking place within these relationships, highlighting what was measured was not important. The focus was on learning and then taking what they learned into other relationships. A company can have only a limited number of significant Learning relationships with other enterprises.

Strategic relationships, upper right quadrant, employ a lot of the most advanced practices—joint forecasting, joint planning, joint strategizing and substantial sharing of confidential information. In Streamlined relationships, lower right quadrant, the process improvements have been particularly refined and the technology interfaces are well established. Not a lot of management time is required to achieve such things as lower costs, vendor managed inventory programs, and so forth.

5. Portfolio Migration

Once a company has determined its optimal relationship portfolio based on its overall business strategy and what it can invest in management time and money, it must work to actively manage migration of its current relationships. For example, companies should be looking for ways to take the results of Learning relationships into other relationships, and also seeking opportunities to take a few selected relationships to new levels of performance through extra management time and investment and by adopting the most advanced practices with New Model characteristics.

As companies seek to migrate selected relationships, they will recognize that they have both successful and unsuccessful relationships. Some relationships are so bad, and perhaps so low in importance, that companies need to find alternatives or discontinue them. Other relationships, while only moderately good, may be important enough to the company to seek various ways to migrate them to the highly successful portfolio.

6. What Leaders Do

To determine which companies were considered leaders in advanced relationships within the consumer-directed supply chains, the 200 study participants were asked who they knew that were particularly good in advanced relationships and in overall supply chain performance, and why they thought this. One hundred and six companies were named by their peers, 46 of which were among the 200 companies included in the study. These 46 companies were designated the "leaders" in the study and were analyzed relative to the non-peer named companies in what ways they differed. For example, leaders in our study were twice as likely, 41 percent of the leaders versus 20 percent overall, to have described relationships that had Strategic characteristics - high investment of time and resources, and many advanced practices.

When the leaders group was broken into manufacturers versus retailers, we found additional things of interest:

- Leading manufacturers have extraordinarily high expectations that their customers will develop partnerships with them. They have a value orientation to advanced relationships and a more productive and intimate way of doing business. They also expect more streamlined ordering so they can plan. And for their best customers, they allocate substantially more time and resources than the non-leaders.

- Leading retailers also showed differences from the rest of the retailers in our study. By six to one, leading retailers want EDI capability. They want suppliers to go the extra mile to help improve their logistics. Leading retailers do not think that suppliers can improve a situation by developing better information systems, per se, or need their supplier to be flexible in exceptional situations. These leaders have already solved those problems. It is the followers that need other enterprises to go the extra mile, be more flexible and fix problems when they occur because they occur often.

7. The Characteristics of Different Relationships

Earlier this year, we analyzed the original data based on the differing characteristics of the four different types of relationships. In the case of what retailers expect of manufacturers, surprisingly, companies in High Touch relationships did not expect honesty and openness, per se, from their manufacturers. Retailers in Strategic relationships needed manufacturers to understand their needs. Retailers wanting EDI capability were also highly centered in the strategic area. And accuracy and high fill rates were also very important for highly strategic retailers. Interestingly though, when we sliced the data again, separating the peer-named leaders and the followers, we saw that leaders in the High Touch and Streamlined relationships are also concerned with accuracy and high fill rate - much more than the followers.

On the manufacturer's side, no matter what type of relationship, they expect honesty and openness from retailers. Help in developing electronic compatibility was more centered in the Strategic relationships, and developing partnerships was important to just about everyone except the High Touch, legacy relationships from the past. When we sliced the manufacturing data to reveal leaders versus followers, we saw that the only group not concerned with honesty and openness were the leaders in Streamlined relationships. Help in developing electronic compatibility was a trait held by the leaders in the lower-investment groups (High Touch and Streamlined), but it is hardly evident among the followers in those two groups. One of the most amazing statistics is that 80 percent of the leaders in Strategic relationships expect retailers to develop partnerships.

Remember that these numbers were compiled using probing, but non-leading, questions. Followers in the Strategic
areas have a very different agenda and a very different kind
of expectation, with far fewer wanting partnerships but far
more wanting excellent forecasting and clearly defined expectations.

What does all this mean? Well, one thing we found out
is that leaders have many more advanced relationships and
fewer unsuccessful ones. They're expanding their Strategic
and Learning relationships as a portfolio strategy, and then
incorporating their relationships and the elements of their
relationships into the context of what they're trying to
strategically accomplish: dramatic top- *and* bottom-line
payouts. The followers have a more stable situation in that
they're not actively migrating relationships as much, and
they have many more unsuccessful relationships.

8. Benefits

When we assessed the different kinds of achieved benefits
among the four types of relationships, we again see some
interesting things. First, increase in sales growth and volume is a primary descriptor of the benefits to those companies that are doing a high degree of measuring and tracking
— Strategic and Streamlined relationships. Those that are
not talking about measures being important are also not
talking about increased sales growth. We know they're
measuring it, but it is not what comes to "top of mind"
when they describe their highly successful Learning and
High Touch relationships. Lower prices are a strategy at
the Strategic level and not particularly in the other relationship categories. Special treatment, stability and loyalty
are not important to the high investment (Learning and
Strategic) relationships, but they are important to the other
two types of relationships.

9. Characteristics of a Successful Alliance

We also asked our respondents to tell us the characteristics of successful relationships or alliances. Planning and strategizing together was very important to all four types of relationships. The EDI or technical capability was important to mainly Streamlined relationships. Process improvement was important to relationships that emphasized measurement - Strategic and Streamlined. Not surprisingly, shared vision and common goals were important to the visionary relationships (Strategic and Learning). They're not just concerned with process improvement or vendor managed inventories, but they want to develop a grand plan. Dedicated teams were highly emphasized in Learning relationships.

10. Emerging Practices

Those companies that are actively adopting the New Model are owing their successful progress to "Currencies of Negotiation," a term credited to William L. Ury and Roger Fisher at Harvard. In the early 1990s, too many manufacturers stepped up and created advanced practices as value-added favors for their customers. These favors would then create problems over time because the exchange between the parties was not equal. For example, many manufacturers made concessions to help customers turn their inventories fast, which would cause most manufacturers to increase their own inventories. Eventually, many manufacturers resented being stuck in these types of situations and became disillusioned because they weren't receiving any value. These manufacturers typically had not rebuilt their entire supply chains upstream so that they would not need to increase their inventories, nor did they seek valuable considerations (Currencies) from their retailers to more than off-set the high inventories.

The New Model relies on companies having a more complete, end-to-end vision of the things of value on both sides and creating a grand plan for the exchange of Currencies of Negotiation. The New Model has companies negotiating and cooperating based on creating mutual benefits throughout an entire supply chain and for the end-of-the-chain consumers.

Information sharing is somewhat controversial for some companies, which have a difficult time thinking about sharing historically very confidential information. While marketing promotion and campaign plans may be easy to share, proprietary cost data may be much more difficult. About half of the 200 companies had no problem with essentially sharing all of these categories listed in Figure 8, while the rest had reservations about at least some of them.

The Challenges

Clearly, trust is a crucial ingredient for advanced relationships - but it is not the only key ingredient. There are other Currencies of Negotiation that have to be coupled with trust and skillfully integrated to help create advanced relationships that then lead to advanced supply chain practices. Advanced relationships must be selectively sought within the context of an overall relationship strategy, advanced practices strategy, and business strategy.

Each of the four types of highly successful relationships has its place, and a company must have a strategy for managing each of the four within its relationship portfolio. Relationships with companies can be targeted for movement within this portfolio, and, in many cases, if the true expectations of the other parties are discovered and taken into account, the relationships can be migrated and upgraded more quickly. The key is to adopt and adapt the New Model, the softer side of the business, and integrate it with the harder side of business. Even leading companies are overlooking, at times, the variety of roles that trust, credibility, openness, or honesty can play in leveraging customer or supplier relationships to even higher performance levels.

Business strategy has to include an end-to-end vision for the entire supply chain. A strong enterprise in a weak supply chain will not be successful. This is why "customer-driven," if not dead, can be very dangerous. It's too easy for companies to focus on serving only their customers, and not their customers' customers, or to focus on suppliers and not their suppliers' suppliers.

Truly advanced relationships are both opportunities as well as threats, because there is a limit to the number of high investment, high payout relationships that any one customer or supplier can have. Once that capacity is consumed, analogous to "share of shelf" limitations in retail stores, a company can be closed out and out of luck. And that is why growth in market shares will increasingly only be available to those companies with a clear relationship portfolio vision and strategy, *and* those that are also swift. You can always take cost out by better practices, but you can't get market growth by better relationship-based practices if there is no room for these relationships.

Finally, developing truly advanced relationships requires companies to take several key steps:

1. Fully and objectively assess the relationship portfolio - which ones are highly successful and which of the four types of relationships are they. Also, which other relationships are important enough to work on even though they are currently unsuccessful?

2. Categorize relationships from both sides - customers and suppliers. The views on both sides will not always match, which raises additional important issues and challenges to be dealt with.

3. Ensure that the internal organization has consistent views of each key relationship.

4. Relate these assessments to the overall business strategy, with particular attention to visionary strategies for the entire end-to-end supply chain. Develop a migration and execution plan so that relationship-based, advanced practices can be successfully and rapidly deployed.

Leaders are doing these things. The result is an effective supply chain that services the ultimate consumer, which thereby yields big payouts for all of the companies in their supply chains.

Trust, is of course, an ingredient in all advanced relationships, but extensive research shows that it must be positioned within an end-to-end strategy to be truly useful in the right context for the right purposes. Otherwise trust is just a stone in an ordinary wall and not a keystone in an extraordinary structure.

CHAPTER V:

Trust at all Levels: A Framework for Strategic Partnering at Hewlett-Packard

Mike Cohn
Manager, Global Sales Programs
Hewlett-Packard

Sherry Kilgus
Director of Marketing
National Account Management Association

CHAPTER V

Company Background

To understand HP's current method of management and how trust was built with its partners, it is first necessary to understand its history and culture and the forces of change which caused HP to adopt its current practices. HP is a $43 billion company that spent $3B on R&D in 1997. Its growth from new products and markets is critical. HP's culture has always been one of working together within the company and fostering an engineering mentality, in which products are being continually developed. The culture strongly supported a "we do it better" theme and an independent, inventing, entrepreneurial spirit. Originally, HP had limited interest in collaborating and forming alliances with other companies, and it adhered to a philosophy of "we can design and build it all."

However, HP began to realize that things don't work this way in the computer field, and this presented an interesting challenge to HP's traditional way of working. A "bolt of lightning" hit in the mid 1980s, and HP made the decision to go to open systems, away from proprietary systems. At the time, it was a second tier player in the computer industry, and senior management determined that the only way to get into open systems was through collaboration. Therefore, HP had to change its culture to move toward collaboration, and thus toward partnerships and alliances. Now, more than a dozen years later, "partnering" is acknowledged as a core competency of HP.

The Move to Industry-Based Sales Organizations

In the early 1990s, HP moved from a geographically-based

sales organization to one based on industry. This decision was made because it is easier to analyze customer needs and provide more complete solutions according to industry. The company can more efficiently focus resources by industry. This industry alignment enabled trust by building relationships in which both companies became very familiar with each others' processes and were able to deliver better service.

Framework for Strategic Partnering

The program had two objectives: 1) to bring the extended field sales organizations together and 2) to build a common mindset/vocabulary about what to do and how to talk to the customer.

Goals. HP's ultimate goal in this process was to enable sales teams to establish strategic relationships with their customers that would help HP to sell more profitably in the future and that result in:

- Long-term business alliances (win/win)
- Strategic positioning of products and services in accounts
- Increased growth/market share
- Lower cost of selling

HP also had an initial objective of becoming a "trusted advisor" to customers. While this was a noble objective, HP was not going to be able to achieve it in every account. HP had to figure out a way to conquer the myth that if it didn't become a trusted advisor, it had failed in an account. HP had to realize that it couldn't be a trusted advisor for all customers, because not all customers want that, or they may want it from someone else.

Team. The team was assembled with people from all major disciplines including quality programs, professional services, strategic big deals, and contracts, in order to analyze the process and determine in which direction to proceed.

Evolution. The process was as follows:
- The team collected current project and partnership agreements to figure out what was working.
- "Winning Themes" were identified.
- A business development process was created that enabled sales teams to:
  1. qualify customer/account relationships today
  2. understand where the relationships can go in the future
  3. build a plan to effectively get there (incorporating "winning themes" while focusing on profitability, minimum risk, and flexibility)
- An implementation methodology was created.
- The methodology was tested at select accounts.
- Success was measured.
- The program was communicated and the sales team trained.
- The program was rolled out.

HP found that the business units that didn't go through this process struggled, because they were trying to love their customers to death. Fundamentally, the role of "trusted advisor" is a mismatch for certain relationships, and until you put the tools and the vocabulary in place to understand that, you tend to over-invest in some customers and become frustrated with their lack of return/response.

Levels of Relationship. Based on this process, HP formulated a 3-tiered model of customer relationships (Figure 1) that is its foundation for supplier/customer relationships today. The levels of relationship are product vendor, value-added supplier, and strategic partner.

Figure 1

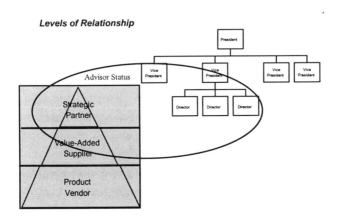

It's okay for customers to be in any one of these three segments. The company simply cannot afford to be a strategic partner with all customers: it does not have the resource capacity, financial capacity, or the tolerance for risk. It also cannot afford to be just a product vendor, because this just results in competing on "speeds and feeds: today's data sheet." Ideally, the company needs to have a portfolio of all three. Regardless of which of the three paths a relationship follows, the two companies must match words with a set of actions, and this must be reflected in the account plan. Also, trust is important at all relationship levels, but it becomes more and more important as companies move through the value-added and toward the strategic partner realm.

Relationship Analysis. A definition of the three tiers of the model follows (Figures 2 & 3). The product vendor relationship is a short-term commitment to buy/sell products based on volume, price, delivery, features and fit. The ultimate goals in this kind of relationship are volume end-user purchase agreements, standard maintenance agreements, and time and materials consulting. The typical characteristics for the product vendor relationship focus on the following:

- Features
- Products and technologies that meet customers' needs
- Facilitating transactions and ease of doing business
- Price and delivery
- Willingness to establish bases for buying and selling products at discount
- Willingness to buy basic support services to guarantee product usability
- Willingness to buy time & materials consulting services
- Operational efficiency (as opposed to customer intimacy)

In the product vendor relationship, the supplier/product may be easily replaced, such as with PCs. The accounts are increasingly "low touch," with channel distribution able to supply more of the customer's needs. There is usually a one-sided win, but since there is mutually low investment between the customer and HP, this model works.

A value-added supplier relationship is a mid-term commitment to gain/add value based on moderate risk, complementary competencies and shared rewards. The ultimate goal in this relationship is a formal business/project agreement with measurements and owners. The typical characteristics for the value-added supplier relationship focus on the following:

- supplier's solution set satisfies customers' needs
- assigned business/project team
- executive sponsorship
- successful implementations
- willingness to make limited commitments & share risks
- sharing of relevant business information
- willingness to share joint successes
- complementary core competencies

Figure 2

Relationship Characteristics

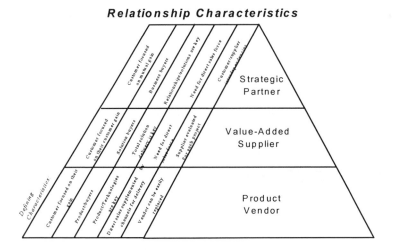

In a value-added supplier relationship, RFPs may still be generated, but typically less often than in a product vendor relationship. Customers are looking for help, and there is increasing "touch." The supplier is focused on customer solutions, and the equation is becoming increasingly balanced. There is mid-term commitment, some shared risk, some core competencies come into play, some joint development, some teamwork, and executive sponsorship for the first time. The relationship is going beyond the transaction level. As you move up the commitment ladder, you need to pull together your team to deliver to the customer. To the extent you are making investments with the customer, it is important to gain commitment from the people who "control the checkbook" who can deliver the resources needed.

A strategic partnership is a long-term business relationship based on shared risk, interdependency and mutual gain. The ultimate goal in this kind of relationship is a formal partnership agreement with measurements and owners. The typical characteristics of a strategic partnership focus on the following:

- A compelling reason to partner
- Dedicated partnership team
- Multilevel executive involvement
- Willingness to make significant business commitments and share risks
- Critical business decisions based on mutual, long-term value-added
- Focus on lower long-term cost of doing business together
- Sharing of critical business information (e.g. early access to technology, business plans, etc.)
- Development of expected outcomes/indicators of success (joint metrics)
- Willingness to promote joint successes
- Integrated TQM sales/support process (customer satisfaction)

In a strategic partner relationship, there is a lot more focus on the relationship and the business, and therefore trust. The risk and the stakes go up on both sides. There is interdependency, mutual gain, shared risk, high trust, and a compelling reason to do business. As you move up the value chain, there is increased risk, value, sharing, and relationship focus. This means that trust becomes essential further up the value chain. There is decreased focus on features, price, the total cost of buying and selling, and the number of suppliers. The key point is that, in committing to a strategic alliance, a company has to have the resources to make it work. Resources may be the limiting factor as to how many alliances can be managed.

Figure 3

Relationship Characteristics

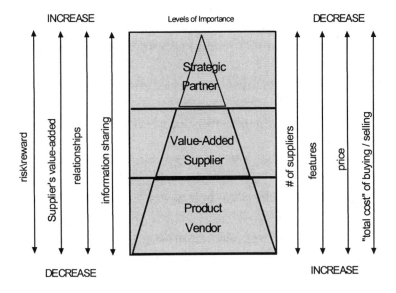

A strategic partnership requires dedicated people. There are no escapes, no excuses, and full accountability. Without a dedicated team, the company will get sucked into its internal infrastructure. There have to be multiple contacts and multiple levels of executive involvement. Life is ugly when relationships are "buyer/seller" and "chairman to chairman." In this scenario, things flow up at the speed of light and come down like a train wreck, and when the train hits, no one wants to hear the details, just 'fix it.' This is why multiple people need to be involved and take accountability.

Account Planning

The next question for HP was how to get to this framework. HP needed to take its formal Account Management Plan (AMP) and factor in where the accounts stood in the relationship triangle. In order to do this, HP looked at sales processes. In the product vendor category, the goal was to get standard volume agreements. In the value-added category, the goal was to get value-added supplier agreements, and to spend more time understanding what drives the customer, the customer's problems, and how to solve them. In the strategic partner category, the goal was to develop sustainable, long-term partnerships, where the needs, processes, and relationship-building aspects are assessed.

In the strategic partner relationship within its account management process, HP came up with a triangle model involving four critical success factors (see Figure 4).

The Role of Trust

In the strategic partner category, *trust* is very important. Contracts can break this trust, since they really define rules for disengaging from a relationship, rather than defining the rules to stay in. Knowing when to write them and how can make a real difference. Thus, in this realm, HP has looked to "memos of understanding," or project agreements, that have often taken the place of standard contracts. This process has helped to build trust with customers because it has fostered better communications and clarified mutual goals between the two parties. Also, HP learned to get contracts people involved in the process much earlier, coaching the team and keeping the company from getting backed into a corner and alienating the customer.

Partnership Success Factors

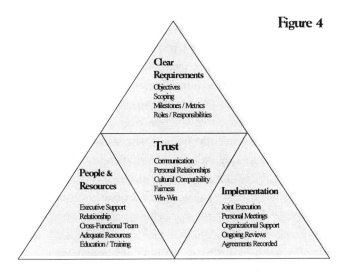

Figure 4

Also, it is important for things to be fair, and not necessarily equal, between customer and supplier. This means that both sides should contribute a *fair* investment and realize a *fair* return. It takes trust to allow this to happen. In addition, adequate resourcing is key to the partnership, with cross-functional teams being increasingly important. These teams provide the authority, the knowledge, the "check book," the capability, and the time needed to make a partnership run successfully.

What HP Learned

The overriding thing that HP learned through this process was that accounts can fall into any of the three levels of relationships – product vendor, value-added supplier, or strategic partner. The key is that resources need to be invested according to where the supplier/customer relationship is today and can be in the future: it's called 'running your business.'

Resource Allocation

Product Vendor Level. At this level, HP pays for the majority of resources involved, since these resources are minimal per customer. The customer-to-sales ratio is relatively high, relative to 'value-added.' Sales are supplemented by support specialists, telesales, channel partners, etc. The supplier funds the work that is done.

Value-Added Supplier Level. As you move up the value chain, it becomes more complicated to fund investments, with more co-funding between partners. Here, the customer-to-sales ratio is closer to 'one to one.' Supplier and customer may co-fund the value-added work done.

Strategic Partner Level. By the time the strategic relationship level is reached, there is much more investment and it is more shared. The customer-to-sales ratio may be much greater than 'one to one' (multiple resources to one customer). Sales are supplemented by project managers and program managers. Supplier and customer co-fund the work done. Here, there is more customization, more technical expertise, and more "value-added" needed. Resources needed are heavily weighed toward the technical rather than the sales resources.

HP learned that it made sense for most of its accounts to

fall in the middle of the triangle, at the "value-added" level. This is where it could most effectively manage the majority of its accounts. At the same time, it could better fund its strategic partnerships where it really needed them, and it could migrate many of its product vendor accounts to the distribution channel where they would be handled most efficiently.

Summary
HP found some key elements in its process of building a framework for strategic partnering:

- Sales team commitment to stronger/broader account relationships

- Contract rep involvement from the beginning

- An "integrated" relationship development team – sales, professional services, support services, contracts, etc.

- Relationship qualification with all three types of account executives – business, IT, and procurement

- Account relationship qualification discussions should take place at the highest level in the account

- Lead with relationship analysis and follow with relationship agreement

HP also found that there are ten key things that are critical to strategic alliances:

1. They evolve.

2. Goals must continually be set and re-set to adapt to change.

3. Customers and suppliers must continually look for the "win/win."

4. Customers and suppliers learn a lot about each other.

5. Things change, and time windows of opportunity open and close all the time, including new market pressures and technology.

6. Many times partners are buying and selling to each other: product going back and forth.

7. It is critical to keep senior management involved.

8. Relationships must be based on trust and honesty, because you can't write it all down.

9. Cultural compatibility is essential.

10. Communication is essential: must have open and regular reviews to tell both the good and the bad news.

CHAPTER VI

JIT II~The Ultimate Customer / Supplier Partnership: Trust & Controls Make It Happen

Lance Dixon
Executive Director
JIT II Education & Research Center

CHAPTER VI

The JIT II business concept, conceived and implemented by Bose Corporation in 1987, is now being implemented in various US corporations – mainly because it is the next logical step in two of today's cutting edge concepts, "partnering" and "concurrent engineering". It also enhances aspects of JIT itself. Accordingly, we are witnessing an evolution in the relationship between "customer and vendor," and the way we conduct business with each other, which are an advance and a win for both companies. JIT II is the ultimate in closeness when it comes to partnering, and trust is inherent within the process because two companies have to trust each other to work this closely and pull it off.

As a benchmark, these observations are based on nine years of such operations at Bose, encompassing nine JIT II vendors and eleven JIT II in-plant vendor personnel addressing 25% of purchased dollar volume of material. The purchased commodities include plastic tooling and parts, metal parts, corrugated packaging, MRO, printing, import functions, and domestic and international transportation. Let me briefly state the basic concepts involved:

- "JIT" is a worldwide-recognized Japanese business technique
- "JIT II" is a registered service mark of Bose Corporation.
- JIT eliminates inventory and vendor and customer work closer together
- JIT II eliminates the salesperson and the buyer, allowing vendor and customer to work closer together.

In practice, a vendor employee sits in the purchasing office of the customer, replacing the buyer and the salesperson. He is empowered to utilize the customer's purchase orders and places orders on himself, in effect. It is important that the existing buyer or planner is transferred to a new position. If downsizing is the goal, it should occur over one to two years by attrition. Working together properly is assured by this approach.

The vendor in-plant person is also empowered to practice "concurrent engineering" from the in-plant location, attending any and all design engineering meetings involving his company product, with full access to customer facilities, personnel, and data.

Reverse EDI is also used when a supplier can look into the customer's MRP system, from his computer halfway around the world, and identify material needed, which becomes the authority to place the order on himself. No in-plant person is required by this approach. In practice, both means are used. The in-plant person is used where a person is best, and computers are used where a person is not needed. Both means can provide authority in the customer system to the supplier, which is the definition of JIT II.

The process brings the vendor "partner" into the plant, full-time, and provides full and free access to customer data, people,. and processes—with an "Evergreen" contract and no bidding rituals. The key element is not only being physically located inside, but to be empowered within the customer purchasing function as the link between the customer's planning department and the vendor's production plant. This requires trust between the vendor and customer. The prior system of 'planner to buyer to salesman to vendor order-taker' is now 'customer planner to vendor in-plant'.

Efficiencies are achieved in both companies in various ways. Today's concept of concurrent engineering says we shall invite our vendors to meet with us and review new product designs for our mutual benefit. The next logical advance is to bring these vendors inside full-time. It places concurrent engineering in-plant, at the customer location, on a full time basis, rather than today's normal practice of "visits."

JIT is advanced and made more effective because the vendor attempting to work from forecasts while outside the customer location moves to a position location inside. From this posture, the in-plant vendor interfaces heavily with planners obtaining and critiquing information with more timeliness and more insight then today's normal practices.

Key Perspectives

The key to considerable improvement in business practices is this relationship and structure that allow in-plant vendor personnel to place customer purchase orders on themselves and allow free access to customer plant and engineering programs full-time. Once this basic and rather substantial act of faith and trust is accomplished, a wide range of daily business activity can be improved beyond today's norms. The JIT II relationship is the facilitator and catalyst for change and improvement to various accepted current business practices in purchasing, planning, engineering, importing and transportation. From the vendor side, JIT II can also be adopted from a sales and marketing perspective as integral to the functioning of a company's marketing and national accounts programs. Many companies are already marketing themselves that way.

Purchasing at Bose

Purchasing at Bose is composed of several functions and sections:

- New production introduction (plastic, mechanical, electronic)
- Plant material purchasing
- Finished goods purchasing
- Corporate purchasing (worldwide coordination)
- MRO, Capital purchasing
- Vendor engineering
- Transportation, international and domestic
- Bose truck fleet operations
- Purchasing departments in Bose plants worldwide

Integration

If you look closely at the organization, you will note the location of JIT II in-plant supplier representatives integrated with various purchasing sections:

- Roadway Express in-plant in transportation
- Procter Inc. Import/Export in-plant in transportation
- Doranco in-plant in mechanical new product purchasing
- G&F Plastics in-plant in corporate purchasing and Bose plant locations
- United Printing in-plant in MRO purchasing and plant locations
- Entex Information Services in-plant in personal computer and software
- SGS-Thomson in-plant in electronics

Operating Improvements to Customer & Supplier

With JIT II, there are various operating efficiencies to both customer and vendor.

Customer:

> Headcount reduction (or additional staff to address other purchasing needs and programs).

> Dramatically improved communication and purchase order placement as customer planner deals directly with vendor plant person. A two-step communication replaces previous four-person route (planner to buyer to salesman to plant person).

> Ongoing material cost reduction as vendor person is also empowered to pursue "concurrent engineering" from in-plant location. Costs are lowered on new and existing product with savings shared. Initial cost levels held firm for years.

> A living, breathing "standards program" as the several vendors sitting in on early design engineering meetings are the ones the purchasing and engineering directors want maximized and designed in. (To the extent that vendor personnel are more plentiful than the previous buying staff, they tend to, in fact, participate earlier and more effectively than "regular" buyers and vendor personnel who don't have the advantage of being in-house).

> Natural foundation for EDI and other administrative savings. Computer terminals and software from vendor tie customer and vendor together. Both work from real time vendor data and have free total data access to each other's company data.

Vendor:

➢ Elimination of salesperson effort (but increased cost of full-time person at customer's location).

➢ Dramatically improved communication and purchase order placement as customer planner deals directly with vendor plant person. A two-step communication replaces previous four-person route (planner to buyer to salesperson to plant person).

➢ Increased dollar volume of business at start of program; increased "critical mass" of business offsets on-site vendor person costs above.

➢ "Evergreen" contract. No end date and no annual rebidding (costs stay at initial level for several years in practice).

➢ Vendor has ability to sell his process and skills directly into engineering. He has the ability to get designed in early in a manner most efficient to his process, tooling, etc.

➢ Increased business from the "customer partner" by being in-house and having free rein to participate in all early engineering sessions and provide input for maximum shared benefit.

➢ Efficient invoicing and payment administration as paperwork reduced and invoices paid in timely manner.

➢ No sales effort and cost as in-house person working jointly at purchase order placement and concurrent engineering is "de facto" the best sales effort.

> Vendor on-site personnel have "dual" career path, can advance in vendor company or job post at Bose after one year.

Daily Working Insight

To better illustrate how all this works, let's follow John Brown, In-Plant Representative from ABC Industries, around for a typical day at Bose. ABC Industries supplies plastic injection molding tooling, plastic parts, and metal parts to Bose, shipping to various Bose plants worldwide.

John starts some days at his plant in Weston, Massachusetts, where he controls various production schedules with a status review of Bose in-process parts. He arrives at the Bose manufacturing plant, where he confers with Fred Smith, the other ABC In-Plant. Fred is heavily involved in the daily planning and ordering of ABC material for this particular Bose plant, using Bose purchase orders from his location in the plant purchasing department.

John arrives at his office in the Corporate Purchasing Department late morning where he confers with the Bose plant material planners and receives related material requisitions. He calls them in to his plant after sign-off by the Bose purchasing manager on an order that exceeds his dollar authorization per order, the same as with any Bose buyer. At one o'clock, he attends a Bose new product project review at the Bose Mountain Headquarters location, gathering information of any importance on parts ABC will be supplying.

Two o'clock brings John into contact with Bose design engineers, who have questions on process possibilities and cost trade-offs on a plastic part and various materials. At three, a quality control issue is addressed with Corporate and Plant Quality personnel. Today, John is leaving early for the airport to fly to the Bose San Luis, Mexico facility, where a new product start-up is to take place with various ABC parts. He is versed in all aspects of the product start-up and possible difficulties, having participated in the pilot production in the Bose Massachusetts plant.

Controls

A frequently asked question is how do you control the dollar flow, parts ordering, and ultimately, the material cost? The in-plant representative operates at a buyer level. The normal controls that the typical purchasing systems and purchasing manager place on a buyer function quite well.

All dollar flow and ongoing material costs are reflected on computer printouts of various cost-tracking programs. All parts have "standard costs" negotiated by purchasing and frozen by accounting for review, controls that are normal and standard practice in most companies. Both companies are happy with material cost levels and the efficiencies both companies have found through the relationship and various procedures described.

The JIT II Customer/Vendor Profile

JIT II concepts can be implemented in a wide range of purchased commodities. The material implemented can be to support "production" and/or "non-production," or so-called MRO materials. The concept works well in either sole-source or multiple-vendor per commodity situations. It should be noted that we only implement one JIT II vendor in a given commodity. Bose has found that it is not a problem to have one "most favored nation" vendor relationship, and still carry on a professional, mutually satisfying, fair relationship with other competing vendors in the same commodity.

Vendor Insight/Profile
The "indicators" for potential JIT II partners will include:

➢ An excellent vendor (the best in a given commodity)

➢ $ volume over $1 million

➢ Current good quality

➢ Substantial number of purchase order transactions

➢ Current good delivery

➢ Evolving technology, but not at a revolutionary change pace

➢ Current good cost levels

➢ Customer company non-trade secret or sensitive technology area

➢ Current good engineering support

The next phase is to open the appropriate discussions with vendor senior management.

Current Status
The Bose trademark (JIT II) has been adopted for use in sales and marketing by a growing number of major corporations. Recently, SGS-Thomson, a world leader in electronics and a long-term business partner with Bose, has acquired the license rights to the JIT II trademark for use in marketing and customer support. They join Marmon/Keystone, BT International, ISA Corporation, Deloitte

& Touche, Tower Division of McGraw-Hill, Roadway Inc.,
Process Products, and a number of smaller corporations. A
number of other major relationships are in process as JIT II
moves from being a US "best practice" to a standard practice.

Several executives from these firms assist us by serving on
the Advisory Board of the Bose JIT II Education & Research
Center. In the US, corporations practicing JIT II in their
purchasing and logistic area include IBM, Intel, Honeywell,
AT&T, Westinghouse, Motorola, Sun Microsystems, Gulf-
stream Aerospace, Foxboro, Lotus, and many others. *Purchasing* magazine says "hundreds, maybe thousands of companies."

The Harvard Business School and Darden Graduate
School have published JIT II case studies that have facilitated the teaching of JIT II in universities worldwide. Recently we have carried out presentations at leading universities and companies in Belgium, France, Canada and Vene-
zuela.

JIT II has been featured in front-page articles in the US
and European *Wall Street Journal* and ongoing worldwide
business periodicals. *BusinessWeek* named Bose one of the
'World-Class Champs' in supplier management. This year
Arthur Anderson has named JIT II a "Best Practice". The JIT
II videotape is used in dozens of University MBA programs
nationally and worldwide, combined with the case study by
the Harvard Business School. The textbook *JIT II: Revolution
in Buying and Selling* has been published by Cahners Publishing.

CHAPTER VII:

Organization-To-Organization Trust: Procter & Gamble / Wal-Mart

Tom A. Muccio
VP Customer Business Development (Wal-Mart)
Procter & Gamble Worldwide

CHAPTER VII

In 1987, Wal-Mart and Procter & Gamble senior management made the decision to change the way they did business together. At the time, their business relationship was badly broken and best characterized as:

- Adversarial

- Transactional

- Internal-process focused and driven

- Relationships and activities managed by buying and selling functions only

The work between the two companies over the last ten years has been an excellent case study on the process of changing a business relationship between companies by "building organization-to-organization trust." Through the ten-year period, the business between the two companies grew from $350 million to almost $4 billion, but it hasn't been without many "speed bumps" along the way.

Learnings

Looking back over the ten-year period, it's easier to see the patterns of what worked and what didn't work than it was when we started up or as we were going along. Our learnings of what worked and what didn't are fairly broad, given the systemic nature of the relationship between Wal-Mart and Procter & Gamble. While some of the issues are not applicable to all companies based on the different size of businesses or different industry conditions, there are a lot of experiences that will have broad reapplication.

Key Learning #1: Decision From Above

Our first area of learning was that this process needed to start with the <u>decision</u>. Senior management of both P&G and Wal-Mart decided that there had to be a better way of conducting business between the two companies than was currently in operation, and they were willing to experiment and sponsor work that was different from what had been done in the past in order to discover that better way.

Key Learning #2: Substance & Scope

The second area of learning was based on substance and scope of the relationship. Wal-Mart was a highly successful retailer with all indications that it would continue that success in the future. P&G was a premier marketer of consumer products, again with the prospect of continuing that into the future. The two companies were already important to each other when the relationship started, and both companies were willing to make investments because the relationship was expected to grow in importance over time. This isn't unlike the investment in the relationship that would be made between marriage partners versus casual acquaintances.

Key Learning #3: Significant Structural Change

Another area of learning was the significant structure change that contributed to building trust. Procter & Gamble was organized on a multi-division basis (P&G had ten different and independent divisions call on Wal-Mart) and didn't have one voice to speak to Wal-Mart; Wal-Mart had different business units that didn't allow for one voice to P&G. The first structural change was to create a Team Leader position at both Wal-Mart and P&G to represent their respective companies in the relationship. This didn't mean that the answers needed to be the same for all the divisions at P&G or all the business units at Wal-Mart. What it did mean was that one voice in each company had to understand the differences and why they were important.

Additionally, the relationship between the two companies was changed from one where the buyer and seller were the predominant communication influences to one that provided multifunctional interface from all the major functions, stakeholders, and enabling groups within both companies (as shown in the figure below).

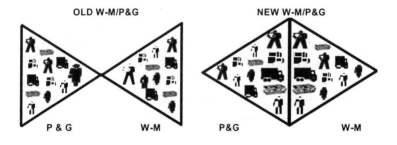

The structural changes enabled better communication and better data flow to make decisions. Therefore, the decisions were better understood, which in turn enhanced the building of organization-to-organization trust. In stepping back and looking at the process, what this says is that the criteria used for developing a partnership is very important.

The Wal-Mart/Procter & Gamble relationship was greatly assisted by:

- Common values

- Similarity of cultures

- Long-term commitment to prospects of both companies

- The realization that both companies had a common customer who was the end consumer

Additionally, going into the relationship, we were aided by the senior management commitment at the top of both of the organizations and a real willingness to see a win/win relationship develop.

Frequently, companies talk about win/win, but they have a great problem accepting the success of the other company when it actually materializes.

Key Learning #4: Managing Expectations

Another area of learning contributing to our ultimate success was the time and effort we spent at the beginning of the relationship to manage expectations within both companies and within the work groups from both companies that would actually do the work.

As an example, we spent time creating the Operating Principles for the work group in such a way that all members felt they were adequately representing the concerns of their own company and how we could disagree without being disagreeable. Following are the Operating Principles that we used to guide our early work:

PROCTER & GAMBLE / WAL-MART INTERFACE TEAM OPERATING PRINCIPLES

I.   *Business Results and Leadership Focus*

- *We will work to improve the profitability of both companies by maximizing opportunities and eliminating unnecessary expenses, but never to the detriment of the ultimate consumer.*

- *We will focus on building the business by applying Total Quality Principles in our work.*

- *We expect strong leadership from everyone on the team. We share the opportunities and responsibilities taking advantage of our individual expertise.*

- *As the lead multifunctional, multidimensional teams in our companies, we recognize responsibility to provide leadership to our companies on how to mold new working relationships between retailers and manufacturers.*

- *We are the advocate for Wal-Mart and P&G within our companies, but in the end we support the business decisions of our respective companies.*

II.   *How We Work*

- *We practice confidentiality of sensitive data within our team. We honor our companies' confidentiality and will not discuss information that is not public knowledge outside the team.*

- *We trust each other's commitment to do the right thing.*

- *We take a total system analytical approach and consult other team members before taking independent action that affects any other function or the other company.*

- *We support each other as individuals and deal with disagreements as business issues rather than personal issues.*

- *We take responsibility to serve as an information resource and keep other team members apprised of important developments within our areas of expertise.*

- *We assume responsibility to keep up to speed with the team when we miss meetings.*

III.   Team Interactions

- *We feel free to challenge existing ways of thinking in all functions and in work done by other groups, etc.*

- *We rely on fairness, our Company policies, and personal ethics for guidance in decision-making.*

- *We create alignment on important issues by seeking consensus. In this process we honor our individual functional and company expertise.*

- *Expenses incurred in team interactions will be split 50-50 on joint expenses or paid by the appropriate team so that no gratuity infractions occur in connection with our team activities.*

- *We treat mistakes as learning opportunities, moving first to control the damage and then to debrief the experience. We*

> maintain a "correction of errors" file to avoid repeating mistakes.
>
> • In the instance when disagreement cannot be resolved by consensus, any team member may exercise the right of appeal to the "next level" manager, in either company, requesting that the problem be revisited.
>
> • We continue the educational process indefinitely, recognizing that learning is just as relevant as the day-to-day business and is a good use of our time.

Other areas that we found were extremely important in managing expectations and keeping ourselves on course included the following:

- A common vision
- Joint objectives
- Extensive data sharing
- Robust internal and external scorecard measurements
- Tangible rewards of success for both companies

We found that the two biggest drivers in creating trust and moving the relationship forward were:

1. Being issue focused rather than position focused

2. Being more concerned about *what* was right than *who* was right

Time and time again, when there were major crossroads in the relationship, if we used these two principles to define how we went forward, we came out at the right place.

As we tried to walk out these Operating Principles, we found a number of practices that when done correctly, facilitated progress, and, when not done correctly, became speed bumps. Those included:

Vulnerability. The way you build trust is by making yourself vulnerable, and the way the other party responds to not taking advantage of you in that vulnerable position confirms the trust and allows it to build to the next level.

Demonstrating early wins. We found there was a lot of low-hanging fruit that could be collected through better communication and a willingness to find a better way. As this happened, it built the confidence of the Team members and encouraged the supporters of this new work within both companies. It also served to identify more and more areas where collaboration would produce excellent results.

We frequently referred to it as "peeling back the onion." Every time we took off one layer of the onion by working together, we found another layer inside that also had excellent potential, but it wouldn't have been discovered without removing the preceding layer.

Reporting success. We found out in our new venture that bad news traveled all by itself; but, if we wanted good news and success to be understood in both companies, we needed to be proactive to get it out and understood in context.

Overcommunication. We found that we needed written, verbal, private, and public communications to help both companies see that the other company was making changes and that by working together, we were getting results that would not be achieved by each company working independently.

Transparency. We learned that by putting problems/opportunities/issues openly on the table and working them without hidden agendas, we were able to make great progress. There wasn't any issue that couldn't be discussed.

Right staffing. We found that there were some people who were much better than others at building this organization-to-organization relationship. The characteristics that seemed to be prevalent in the best Team members were their openness and willingness to think about situations differently. They were trusted internally, had strong functional skills, had the ability to think well, and were all good communicators.

Ability to test. Frequently we would get into a situation where there was a difference of opinion, and the only way we could move forward was to agree to some type of a test with well-defined success criteria. This enabled us to get additional data to know which direction to take next.

Ability to say no. Both companies needed to have the right to say no on some issues because sometimes, regardless of how hard we worked, it just wasn't a win / win situation.

Key Learning #5: Tools for Success
Along the way, we also identified a number of tools or practices that helped us work better and faster. Those included:

Emotional bank accounts. From time to time, one company or the other had to write a "hot check" on the relationship. Therefore, both companies tried to maintain high emotional bank account balances with each other, thus there were always funds to cover the "hot check", provide time to work the issues, and prevent them from recurring or becoming long-term roadblocks.

Co-creation. Whenever we worked together to co-create an idea, we built more commitment to seeing it happen. Almost without fail, we ended up with better plans.

Broadening ownership. We found it highly productive to broaden ownership of the work that was being done so that individuals in all functions and at all levels in both companies were able to see the progress and the benefit to each company individually, and to the various functions and business units within both companies.

Confidentiality agreement. We asked all Team members to sign a confidentiality agreement. This became a good tool for on-boarding every new Team member and helping him or her to understand the importance of confidentiality in the working relationship. It also encouraged them, within this particular area, to ask for permission in advance rather than forgiveness after the fact. The confidentiality agreement was an insurance policy for senior management in both companies to share data, future plans, etc., when that had not been the practice in the past.

Additional Insights

I don't want to give the impression that there was a magic formula or yellow brick road and that once you stay on that, you never have to deal with problems again. Even while the trust and improved working relationship were being developed by those actually doing the work, we frequently had to agree to disagree in a particular area without letting that area bog down the entire relationship.

Additionally, we had to learn to deal with "holy grail" issues within both companies that were very sensitive and not subject to change or negotiation without major "positioning" before the conversation started. Examples of these included P&G's position on private labels and Wal-Mart's position on EDLP pricing.

There was also a group of individuals within both companies who continued to discount the progress that was being made and continued to look for information to reinforce "old tapes." Frequently, these were middle managers whose recognition and reward systems were negatively affected by a short-term decision that the Team made, even though the decision would ultimately result in a better decision or outcome for one or both companies in the long term.

Our standard joke was that the problem with recognition and reward systems is that they work, and you can't ask someone to do one thing and reward them for different behavior. You will almost always get the result that you're rewarding.

On the positive side, we saw time after time that conflicts led to growth. Each of the two companies had strong core competencies to bring to the party, but those strong core competencies tended to push the other party outside their comfort zone. When we learned to play to each other's strengths and be issue-focused rather than position-focused, the conflicts turned to business builders.

We also found it important to make heroes in both companies of those individuals who took risks and stepped out to support new behaviors or new directions. We used every opportunity to change the recognition and reward systems so that the right behavior was rewarded.

Speed Bumps Along the Way

The biggest detrimental factors to building this organization-to-organization trust include the following:

1. *Wrong people.* Every time we made a staffing mistake and had someone who was inflexible or too internally focused, it set the trust levels back at a rate that was 2-3 times faster than it had taken to build.

2. *Inconsistent behavior.* We found that while each company has their own strategy, there are occasionally times when they behave differently than their strategies, and that's typically the result of short-term competitive pressures. Every time that happened in either company, "the loyal opposition" to the relationship in the other company would take great pleasure in pointing out the inconsistency versus the stated strategy.

   We finally concluded that organizations, like people, need to be given enough space to have the occasional "bad day" or to occasionally behave in ways that are not pure from a strategic standpoint.

3. *Surprises.* This is an area where each party has a different understanding of what's going to happen and when, and the action by the other party is an affront or embarrassment. We found over the years that we could handle any kind of problem or difficult issue, but negative surprises almost always were interpreted as a violation of trust.

4. *People turnover.* Continuity in successful business-to-business relationships is not adequately understood by most corporations. If they were, recognition and

reward systems would validate and encourage more continuity.

5. *Internal insensitivity.* Many times individuals within one or the other company made short-term decisions that were detrimental to the trust relationship because their recognition and reward system encouraged internal alignment without sufficient consideration for external alignment. Typically, there was no investment on their part in getting the relationship to its current level, and there was no reward for them in the short term for maintaining or building that relationship.

6. *Bully's loop.* This is a variation on internal insensitivity and comes about when higher ranking members of management are so used to getting their own way internally that the thought of another company challenging their desires is unthinkable. This leads to the famous, "Just tell them that's our policy and, if they don't like it, they can do business with someone else."

7. *Short-term thinking.* Just like in any personal relationship, it's important to ask whether the short-term advantage that can be gained by a particular action is worth the potential damage and long-term consequences to the relationship. We often say that nine times out of ten, the individuals who try to get the last apple on the top of the tree end up getting impaled by a tree limb!

8. *Contracts versus principles.* There's nothing more uncomfortable than finishing an open and candid dis-

cussion on business directions and agreeing on a course of action, only to find that a detailed legal contract is in place that impedes the progress of execution.

The contracts are always written to protect against the most nefarious offenders in the past, rather than to deal with a set of principles based on a trusting relationship. The irony is that very seldom would a company sue its important business partner over the violation of the contract, yet the existence of the contract and the negotiations around it are real drains on building a more trusting relationship.

Advice

When asked what pieces of advice I would give to two companies looking to build systemic trust between their organizations, I encourage them to:

⇒ **Count the cost** before you actually start to build the relationship. Be very clear on how much you're willing to invest, how much you're willing to change your methods of operation, and how much you're committed to establishing the relationship. Again, it's not unlike the difference between a casual relationship and one that's a marriage or family relationship. Jumping in the deep end of the pool is not the best way to teach swimming. All it will lead to is a residual of non-sinkers!

⇒ You'll never get a return on investment if you're unwilling to **make the investment**.

Establishing trust between companies is not easy, is often fragile, and requires significant maintenance to sustain. However, having lived the benefits for the last ten years, I can't believe there's any better way to do business.

CHAPTER VIII

Managing the Extended Enterprise™: An Exercise in Trust

Dave Pearce
Supervisor Continuous Improvement Team
Chrysler

CHAPTER VIII

The trademarked term **Extended Enterprise™** is fast becoming the way Chrysler conducts its daily business. Chrysler feels that its **Extended Enterprise™** concept is the next step in supplier relationships for all sales, service and manufacturing groups.

A major key to the success of any company is how strong its supply base is and how it continues to push the envelope of current practices. Such is the focus of Chrysler's Extended Enterprise concept. With the automotive companies closing the gaps in quality, design and customer satisfaction, the next distinct advantage will be the company with the strongest supplier support system. The old practice of treating suppliers as subordinates can no longer be accepted. We must treat them as equals and depend on their expertise to help make us stronger. Trust is inherent in this process.

This chapter will be presented in two sections. The first will cover Chrysler's outlook and philosophy in working with suppliers. The second section will highlight a joint activity involving the Becker Group, Chrysler's Windsor Assembly Plant and a large cross-functional team from the Chrysler Technical Center.

Part I

In the late 1980s, Chrysler recognized that changes in supplier relationships were a must, not only to survive, but also to gain a competitive advantage over other automobile manufacturers. Chrysler management had many discussions with supplier management to better understand how they could work as a team. Suppliers became an extension of the Chrysler employee base with extensive knowledge of their product. One outgrowth of this activity is the SCORE (Supplier Cost Reduction Effort) program which focuses on sharing savings for all involved. This philosophy fostered supplier partnering and sharing of not only cost reduction ideas, but also product and process improvement suggestions.

The ultimate goal for all involved parties is to delight the final customer. To meet this goal, the entire supply chain must be reviewed, from raw materials through dealer delivery. The groups must look at the total system to minimize cost to the ultimate consumer. This whole scenario must result in a win-win situation for all involved. As partners, all must improve their business situation and continue to grow and improve.

A result of the teamwork may mean that some first tier suppliers become second tier in some instances. This results in a more blended supply base in which tier relationships are not always black and white, but may become blurred or gray. This truly tests the partnership aspect of the OEM and the supplier. Once again, it must be to the advantage of all to change relationships to benefit the final customer. Suppliers must also participate earlier in the development process, which requires trust, as much of the information is still confidential. As team members, suppliers may be on a team with someone that may be a direct competitor on another product. This can be a very testing situation, but in the interest of all, egos are left at the door.

At Chrysler, the suppliers are fully integrated into the platform teams during the development process. This is critical to the fastest possible launching of vehicles with the latest technological innovations and highest quality.

One of the tools which exemplifies Chrysler's partnering philosophy is "SCORE". Chrysler associates will work with suppliers to improve process, product or business practices in the interest of cost reduction, quality improvement and customer satisfaction. Suppliers are responsible for many of the ideas that have helped Chrysler improve internal business practices. It is sometimes difficult when a supplier tells a customer that he can improve, but the idea of "not invented here" is not the issue it once was. It sometimes takes an outsider to point out better ways of doing business. Books could be written about the Chrysler philosophy on partnering with the enterprise and SCORE. Articles appear almost weekly in current periodicals, and companies consistently benchmark the SCORE program.

Part II

An actual example of the Extended Enterprise™ concept is a joint activity with Chrysler and the Becker Group, a major interior component supplier to Chrysler. When the word "we" is utilized in this portion of the text, it will imply Chrysler and Becker. During public engagements, Chrysler and Becker speak as one. This has been an excellent lesson in partnering for all involved. Becker is just one example of teaming with the enterprise to the benefit of all, with the specific focus on the ultimate customer.

There are prerequisites required to support any joint supplier/customer continuous improvement activity. Following are a few issues to be discussed prior to agreeing on any activity:

1. There will be no employees laid off due to this activity. For the Windsor - Becker workshop, this meant not only for the supplier, but also for the Windsor Assembly plant. It is critical that employees view this activity as non-threatening to their jobs in order to maximize their support and participation. If process improve-

ments warrant manpower reduction, then the employ-ees must be utilized in another function or "re-deployed."

2. Once people join the team, they leave their company, and especially their rank, behind. All people have equal say, whether CEO or line worker, customer or supplier. This is the only way to make this activity successful.

3. Everyone must be open and honest. They must trust each other. All cards must be on the table. If there is an issue on either side, it must be discussed and understood by all.

4. This is not just another "study" activity. Facts and data will be gathered and the best possible decision will be made based on available information. Then it's time to "Just Do It" and implement the agreed upon changes. (By the way, the 'Just Do It' term was utilized by a Japanese company as a workshop philosophy before it was picked up by the shoe manufacturer.)

As mentioned above, issues must be discussed. An issue with the Chrysler organization is, in fact, its own organization. Within Chrysler are three separate, but integral, groups that are involved in continuous improvement:

- The Continuous Improvement Department-works with outside suppliers

- Material Supply-handles delivery, ordering, containers

- The Chrysler Operating System Department (COS) includes manufacturing operations and works with

Chrysler plants to implement lean manufacturing techniques.

These groups all have the same goal: to improve efficiency while assuring the highest possible quality and customer satisfaction. Yet they had not worked jointly on any single issue until the Windsor-Becker workshop. Each group had focused in its own area that had brought about great results, but nothing compared to combining the efforts of the three on a specific issue. Let us assure you, this is the first of many joint activities with the three groups.

Throughout the Windsor-Becker project, many departments from all the groups were deeply involved. The initial group for the first workshop activity consisted of approximately 50 people. The first task was to narrow the focus of the project. This was done at the Windsor facility with three days of intense fact-finding and planning, much of which took place right on the plant floor. The scope of such workshops must be set up in bite size pieces rather than taking on the whole plant at one time. As a group, we decided that two areas could be addressed with good payback and limited scope. The two products chosen were the bolster and the D/pillar garnish. We split the group in half to address the two parts. A description of these two products follows.

Bolster

The Windsor Assembly Plant builds minivans (approximately 1500 units per day on a three-shift operation). The best description of a bolster is the handle area attached to the inside of the interior quarter panel trim (the area on which you rest your elbow). Each vehicle requires two parts in some combination, depending on the vehicle configuration. There are also 45 separate part numbers. A material handler picked the parts, put them in pairs and sequenced them for assembly line installation. In total, inventory of individual parts ranged from two weeks to two months. Operators walked miles per day to pick the parts and too much manpower was required. If the assigned operator was absent, it was extremely difficult to train a replacement. If a quality problem was discovered, it was very difficult to react quickly due to inventory and replacement time.

With these problems identified, the bolster team decided their goal was to deliver the parts in pairs in sequence to the line from the supplier facility.

D/pillar Garnish

D/pillar garnish is the plastic trim around the interior edges of the rear liftgate opening of a minivan. Two issues instantly came to the surface as the group began to investigate these components:

⇒ At Becker, the mold makes a left and right-hand part at the same time. The parts are then separated and packed by part number. When the part is received at Windsor, the first operation is for a material handler to pick a left and right part and deliver them to the line in sequence. The issue was the communication between Windsor Assembly and Becker. Why build in pairs, separate, and then put back in pairs? This caused additional operations at both Becker and Windsor.

⇒ At Textron, who supplies some of the D Pillars (as well as some of the bolsters), the molds were made to produce two left or two rights, not one of each together. Why two different tool configurations?

With these issues identified, the D/pillar team decided their goal was to deliver the D/pillar garnish moldings in pairs in the same container. This would not lessen the overall floor space, but would cut the walk distance of the material handler by almost half. This would save manpower at both the supplier and Windsor.

Next Steps

As the groups began to develop their plan, an amazing phenomenon occurred. The groups progressed through the stages of teaming (forming, storming, norming and performing) and really began to gel. It was very interesting to see this take place since all the different groups of people involved had not worked together before. It happened not only with Chrysler groups, but also between Chrysler and supplier, and even between suppliers.

With the primary problems identified and the goals set, there were some major issues to address, most of which had not been solved before. Following are some of the bolster issues that were overcome:

⇒ Multiple shipping locations (Figures 1 & 2). Windsor had to communicate and coordinate with four shipping locations for bolsters - two from Becker and two from Textron. It was decided that one Becker facility would become the sequencing point and the other three facilities would ship to that Becker facility. This required changing logistics routes and coordinating shipping requirements. Also, Becker had to develop a sequencing operation that could support the needs of Windsor.

⇒ Timing was a major issue. The total time from the vehicle leaving the Windsor paint area until the bolsters had to be installed was only 1.5 hours. The team had to find a way to address this issue. With the cooperation of the union employees, the bolster installation point was moved from the Trim assembly area to the Chassis area. In the Chassis area, components like axles, springs, prop shafts, etc., are installed. It was a new idea for this area to install a cosmetic, interior part like the bolster. The cooperation was outstanding. This change allowed a broadcast window (time from paint to installation point) of approximately five hours. This made the sequencing operation possible. To explain the process: as the vehicle leaves the paint area, a signal is sent to the supplier of what component is required. The supplier must load (or in some cases build) the correct part into a rack, load the rack on a truck, deliver the rack to the assembly plant, unload the rack and deliver it to the line in time to install it to the correct vehicle. With all the variables, this is not as easy as it sounds.

The next activity was for both teams to meet at Becker in Sterling Heights to fact find and develop the detailed plan for implementation on the supplier end. The two teams then consisted of about 30 people.

Establishing one location for sequencing was no small task. This area was set up at the Becker Sterling Heights location. This required physical plant changes as well as developing the communication system with Windsor. The communication system had to broadcast the parts in sequence and notify Becker of additional issues like sequence changes, damaged parts or defective parts. This is critical to the ongoing success of the system.

New containers had to be developed to support this activity. The sequenced bolster containers would only be used for delivery of in-sequence parts from Becker Sterling Heights to Windsor Assembly. Three issues were critical:

1. Container design and fabrication. The normal timing for this activity was about ten weeks. We had prototype racks delivered during the activity at Becker, with a delivery date promised less than three weeks after testing for the required number of racks. The racks were good initially, but required modification for long term durability. This was extremely fast for a rack program from concept to implementation. Initially, people said it could not be done, but with the rack supplier as part of the team, anything is possible.

2. Logistics routes for the trucks had to be completely restructured. One reason for selecting Becker Sterling Heights was that additional Becker-built components could also be carried by the same trucks to maximize the loads. This was also set up very quickly and ready to run by the end of the workshop.

3. Coordination and communication were key to this activity being successful. When one of the Becker trucks arrived at Windsor, it was unloaded live (trailer still connected to the tractor) instead of being dropped off to be pulled in and unloaded later. The parts are then taken directly to the line. This is not the normal type of receiving activity for parts, so all the material handling and trucking personnel had to be trained and fully understand how these parts were to be handled.

A key to this activity was the leadership and facilitation role played by the Continuous Improvement group. While maintaining objectivity, the group had to assure forward progress while looking out for the best interest of all parties. This is not an easy task, especially when there are strong personalities and leaders in the groups. Also, it is difficult to keep the various groups involved, especially when issues arise back at the office or plant. The focus must be maintained to meet established timing deadlines with high goals.

Measurable Results

Revenue:

Inventory reduction	$72,644 one-time savings
Reduce scrap (excessive handling)	$ 1,300 per year
Manpower savings (Windsor) 2 per shift x 3 shift =6 x $50,000 per year	$ 300,000 per year
Free up productive assembly plant floor space: 5,000 sq.ft. x $125/sq.ft.=	$625,000
Reduction in expendable containers due to returnables	$426,062

*Error proof assembly line operator decisions reduced to 1
*Receive parts from one location, previously four

Costs:

Becker - labor, transportation,
equipment, floor space   -$932,250

Overall Savings   *$460,000 per year*

Other benefits

1. Competitive suppliers working as partners - mixed Tier I and II roles

2. Joint participation from CAW, UAW and Teamsters

3. Developed sequenced parts delivery system across international border (US & Canada), which is much more complicated and difficult than locally.

4. Reduced complexity at Windsor for operator decision-making.

5. Leveraging best practice sharing which will be a model for other activities.

6. Turned "can't do" into "can do" attitudes for all participants and people outside the teams who did not believe this could be accomplished.

7. Trust for long term partnering: Windsor/ CTC / Becker / Textron / UAW / CAW / Teamsters—this is without a doubt one of the greatest benefits.

Follow up activities

Although the activity is already viewed as a success and many benefits have been gained, there are still issues that have not been completed. Even as the few open issues are finalized, the opportunity for further improvement will always be there. While the sequencing area has been improved, all areas still must be reviewed for continuous improvements. Issues that are still in process include:

- Implementation of one piece flow on D pillar at Becker and Textron
- Revising bolster manufacturing to build in-sequence to Windsor
- Kaizen sequencing area to improve efficiency

Lessons Learned

Chrysler learned to create a model for itself and its suppliers. This model consisted of the following:

- Focus on systems vs. individual components
- Keep activities simple, small and focused
- Look at sourcing, location, strategy and philosophy
- Focus on the customer - plant and supplier interface
- Understand tooling requirements and specifications
- Review product plan for complexity - reduce and standardize parts whenever possible
- No barrier is too big to overcome - especially with an extended team
- Demonstrate patience and perseverance
- Build win-win scenarios
- The importance of TRUST can not be over emphasized

Following is a quote from a Becker representative:

"Our customers expect us to focus on waste elimination. If we don't do it someone else will—and we will lose those customers."

Conclusion

This whole activity is based on improving the competitive position of both the OEM and the supplier. In the eyes of Chrysler, this activity is just the tip of the iceberg for Extended Enterprise™ work. Utilizing such lean thinking mentality, Chrysler and its suppliers will gain distinct advantage over the competition. This will also lead to higher customer satisfaction through improved quality, cost and delivery.

CHAPTER IX:

How NAMs Can Build and Maintain Customer Trust

Joseph Cannon, Ph.D.
Assistant Professor Marketing
Colorado State

Patricia Doney, Ph.D.
Associate Professor Marketing
Florida Atlantic University

Mike Pusateri
Vice President Interactive Sales & Marketing
Marriott

CHAPTER IX

Growth in national account management programs and the National Account Management Association (NAMA) are proof of the increased importance large customers have for many business firms today. The old 80:20 rule has changed, with many firms finding that an even smaller percentage of their customers provide a greater share of their business. The strategic importance of these key customers leads many firms to seek new ways to foster customer satisfaction and commitment to long-term relationships.

One of the primary tactics for getting closer to individual customers is to learn how to best serve and support them – with the ultimate goal being to increase the customer's loyalty and the seller's share of the customer's business. However, many selling organizations are finding that building closer relationships with customers is not easy. Buyer/seller relationships often have a history of being adversarial and built on mutual distrust. Buyers focus on negotiating the lowest price from sellers. Sellers, on the other hand, concentrate on generating sales revenue and moving volume – often without concern for whether the products and services they sell serve the customer's best interests. To counter these perceptions, many selling firms have developed national account management programs to build closer, more trusting relationships with key customers.

This chapter explains how national account managers (NAMs) can develop and nurture more trusting relationships with their customers. We begin by making a case for the importance of having customers trust NAMs and supplier firms. Next, we integrate academic and practitioner perspectives on trust, and provide a definition of trust that focuses on the role trust plays in a national account selling context. Then, we describe five different cognitive processes NAMs can use to build customer trust. We finish by discussing the implications of these trust-building processes for national account management practice.

Why Should We Care if Customers Trust NAMs?

Academic researchers and practicing NAMs have come to recognize the benefits of building trusting relationships. It is well known that customer trust forms the foundation for customer loyalty. Customers who trust NAMs and supplier firms plan to keep buying from them in the future. Trusted NAMs and suppliers also have an edge in competitive bidding situations. The bottom line is more cross-selling opportunities, and the chance to become the preferred supplier in situations where customers typically rely on multiple sources of supply.

Another benefit of building trusting relationships is that customers are much more willing to cooperate with NAMs or supplier firms they trust. By working more cooperatively together, buyers and suppliers can develop new products and services, lower the costs of doing business, and learn more about current and emerging markets for their products. Also, marketing plans can be implemented much more effectively when buyers and sellers collaborate. This is particularly important when the customer is a retailer or distributor, and joint marketing programs are key to sales effectiveness.

Finally, the nature of the NAM/customer interaction is completely changed when the relationship is based on trust. Less of the NAM's efforts are directed toward "selling," because trusting customers are more accepting of the NAM's ideas. This leaves more time to assess the customer's needs and teach the customer. Since trusting customers listen more openly to the NAM's ideas and feel comfortable sharing proprietary information, the NAM can tailor products and services to best meet the customer's current and future needs.

What Is Trust?

It is surprising to see just how many different definitions of trust academics and practitioners use. In the academic community, trust has been studied in social psychology and sociology, as well as in the more applied fields of economics, marketing, and organizational behavior. Researchers agree on the importance of trust, but little else. Each discipline provides a different perspective, based on the application of trust in the particular field. Among practitioners the concept of trust has long been important, whether it involves customers or employees – but here too, "trust" is broadly defined and used in many contexts.

There does seem to be general agreement that some degree of risk is needed to provide a test of trust. Without risk, trust serves little purpose since not much is at stake. Risk generally stems from uncertainty about an important future outcome, or because one party is highly dependent on another party. These conditions are often met in a national account setting, where buying firms typically purchase large quantities of products, often with customized services and support from a supplier. Risk results from the buyer's uncertainty over whether the supplier's products and services will perform as promised. The risk is magnified when the purchase has important consequences for the decision-maker and/or the buying firm. If the supplier fails to live up to its promises, the buyer is vulnerable to the consequences of making the wrong choice.

To incorporate the diverse perspectives on trust in a national account selling context, we define customer trust of a NAM (or her firm) *as the customer's willingness to rely on the NAM (her firm) and to take action in circumstances where such action makes the customer vulnerable to the NAM (her firm)*. In other words, trust involves a customer's assessment of a NAM's or supplier firm's trustworthiness, as well as a willingness to act on this belief in the face of risk.

How Does a Customer Come to Trust a NAM or Supplier?

But how does a buyer develop enough trust in a seller to rely on that seller in a situation that is potentially risky for the buyer? For example, under what conditions will a customer place itself at risk by sharing confidential information with a NAM, purchasing an untested product, or accepting the NAM's estimate of cost savings to be realized by adopting new practices? Our perspective on trust focuses on the cognitive processes, or rational evaluations, a buyer uses to determine the trustworthiness of a NAM or supplier firm. In reviewing the academic literature and relating it to national account selling, we identified five different cognitive trust-building processes:

- calculative process
- prediction process
- intentionality process
- capability process
- transference process

Table 1 summarizes each process, and lists several behaviors of NAMs and characteristics of supplier firms that can contribute to forming trust via a particular process. Since customers may interpret some of these behaviors and characteristics in a number of ways, many of them have been associated with more than one process. In the rest of this section, we "flesh out" each trust-building process and its associated factors.

Table 1 Trust-Building Processes, Factors and Behaviors Which Invoke Each Process	
Trust-Building Process	*Factors and Behaviors Which Invoke the Trust-Building Process*
Calculative: Customer calculates the costs/rewards of a NAM or supplier firm acting in an untrustworthy manner	-a supplier firm's reputation -a supplier firm's size -a supplier firm's willingness to customize -a supplier firm's sharing of confidential information -length of relationship with supplier firm -length of relationship with NAM
Prediction: Customer develops confidence that a NAM or supplier firm's behavior can be predicted	-length of relationship with supplier firm -a NAM's likability -a NAM's similarity to people in the buying firm -frequent social contact with NAM -frequent business contact with NAM -length of relationship with NAM
Intentionality: Customer evaluates the NAM or supplier firm's motivations	-supplier willingness to customize -supplier confidential information sharing -NAM likability -NAM similarity -frequent social contact with NAM
Capability: Customer assesses the NAM or supplier firm's ability to fulfill its promises	-NAM expertise -NAM power in his own firm -NAM's past performance
Transference: Customer draws on "proof sources," from which trust is transferred to the NAM from the supplier firm, or vice versa	-supplier firm reputation -supplier firm size -trust of supplier firm -trust of NAM

According to the economics literature, trust primarily involves a *calculative process* where one party estimates the costs and/or rewards of the other party cheating or staying in the relationship. If the benefits of cheating do not exceed the costs of being caught (factoring in the likelihood of being caught) it is contrary to the other party's best interest to cheat and the party can be trusted. For example, a buyer might calculate that a supplier firm with an excellent reputation has too much to lose – that hard won reputation – to act "untrustworthy."

When trust in based on the calculative process, one party banks on the fact that the other party will do what they say they will do, because they fear the consequences of doing otherwise. For example, a customer firm may knowingly pay a supplier firm premium prices to assure high levels of quality. Essentially, the buyer raises the costs of cheating, since suppliers caught acting "untrustworthy" risk losing highly profitable future business from the customer. A selling firm can also raise the costs of cheating by increasing its own switching costs. Sharing confidential information with customers or customizing products and services – something sellers are often reluctant to do – raises the stakes if the customer should defect to another supplier. On the up side, however, buyers "calculate" that such sellers can be trusted.

The *prediction process* of developing trust relies on one party's ability to forecast another party's behavior. Trust is established based on past history – through repeated interaction, one party gathers enough information about the other party's prior behavior and promises to assess whether or not their behavior is predictable. If it is reasonable to assume that future behavior will mirror the past, trust based on prediction is conferred.

It is easier to establish trust using the prediction process when two parties have done business together for a long time, because the buyer has had more opportunities to observe the seller's behavior. In fact, the broader the range of situations in which the two parties interact, the easier it is for the buying firm to judge the supplier and NAM under unusual circumstances. Thus, frequent business and social contact between members of the buying and selling firms helps to establish trust by means of the predictability process – providing a strong rationale for T&E.

Trust may also emerge through the *intentionality process*, where one party interprets the other party's words and behaviors in order to determine its motives in exchange. Buyers are more likely to trust NAMs and suppliers they believe have their best interests at heart. Not surprisingly, trust is unlikely to develop if the NAM or supplier firm is thought to harbor exploitative or selfish intentions. Thus, to develop trust via the intentionality process, NAMs or supplier firms must demonstrate, through words and deeds, that they can be trusted.

For example, as the NAM and customer interact socially or the customer comes to like the NAM, the NAM's actions provide proof that the NAM is sincerely concerned about the customer. Customizing products and services or sharing confidential information with customers also sends a strong signal that the supplier firm and NAM will not jeopardize the relationship by acting in an untrustworthy way. Finally, when customers perceive NAMs to be similar to them, it is easy for them to figure out the NAM's motives – since they would be presumed to be similar to the customer's own.

The *capability process* involves one party's determination that another party can meet its obligations. For trust to form via the capability process, a customer firm must establish that the supplier firm actually has the ability to do what the NAM says it will do, by the scheduled time. Trust based on capability is important, because while customers may believe that suppliers have the best intentions, they can't rely on suppliers or NAMs whose ability to deliver on promises is questionable.

For example, a NAM may promise the customer prompt delivery, despite a supply being on allocation due to shortages. Yet a customer who doubts whether a NAM has the clout needed to move its order up in the queue would be reluctant to trust the NAM's word. NAMs judged to be expert — in their knowledge of products and processes, and in the customer's industry — invoke customer trust based on the capability process, because they can be trusted to accurately assess the supplier firm's ability to meet the customer's needs.

Finally, trust may develop through the *transference process*, where one party's trust of another individual, organization, or institution transfers to a lesser known party or entity (such as a NAM or supplier firm new to the customer). Conversely, "distrust" may also be transferred if a party lacks other pertinent information. For example, a person's past experience with untrustworthy automobile or insurance salespeople often results in an initial state of distrust.

In a buyer/seller context, the most frequent source of transference would be when the customer has considerable experience with a NAM or supplier firm, but not with both. In such cases, trust (or distrust) is transferred from the known entity to the unknown entity. For example, a new salesperson representing a highly trusted supplier firm benefits from the buyer's past experience with the supplier firm. A supplier firm with an excellent reputation might benefit from trust transferred through favorable "word-of-mouth." Finally, trust might be transferred through a job title — for example, a NAM who is also a Vice President, might be more trusted than a NAM without such a prestigious title.

As previously indicated, some factors may invoke multiple trust-building processes. For example, frequent contact with a NAM may invoke the prediction process by helping the customer more accurately predict the NAM's behavior. Or, the customer may interpret frequent contact as an indication of the NAM's genuine interest in the buying firm's welfare, thereby invoking the intentionality process. Thus, each cognitive process represents a different pathway to trust.

Implications for Account Management

Our framework provides insights to NAMs and supplier firms on how to build and maintain customer trust. This may require a variety of strategic changes both at the account and firm levels. In the next several sections, we present ideas on how to link the trust-building processes to national account programs to establish profitable long-term relationships with customers.

Sales Process

Often in the development of NAM sales programs, the steps and processes are static. In other words, the organization attempts to wrap its functional expertise in a value-added service for its more strategic accounts. These are documented in a cookie cutter package for both NAM and customer to replicate year after year. The flaw in this strategy is highlighted by the calculative process and the intentionality process, both of which suggest that trust may be based on the customer firm's perception that the supplier is willing to make changes on its behalf. Therefore, a supplier would be well advised to place greater emphasis on delivering value around the customer's process relative to its own – an extremely difficult thing to do. Most firms are organized around discipline functions, and the pipeline of information available to them regarding how the customer buying cycle works is virtually nonexistent.

Moreover, there is little or no information on how the customer perceives the market conditions for buying. Therefore, it is not surprising that many of the most successful NAMs are the ones who have convinced their own organization to make internal changes in static processes in response to customers' requests. This not only implies that some customized work on the seller's part is needed for each customer, but also that each buying organization itself is in a dynamic environment requiring process re-engineering as a part of its normal value-based activities.

The bottom line is that the principles of both the calculative and intentionality processes suggest that the NAM sales process has to be a very dynamic, customer-focused system. However, the NAM's ability to be successful here is somewhat relative to the selling organization's culture, systems, and customer orientation. For example, companies vary greatly in their willingness to share confidential information, particularly in the hi-tech arena. Companies like Compaq, HP, IBM and Microsoft all have completely different views on the sharing of confidential data between customers, suppliers, and distributors. Thus, formal and informal company policies can impact the NAM's ability to establish a competitive advantage through trust building activities.

Integrating Trust-Building Processes into Sales Strategy

The trust-building processes should be key considerations when developing a national account sales strategy. For example, the transference process suggests that it is wise to assess the selling firm's size, market share, and reputation before settling on a sales strategy. The stature of the supplier firm determines how much effort a NAM should invest in activities which ensure that the supplier is included in the buyer's consideration set, versus how much time should be devoted to managing and defending direct competitive assessments made by the buyer. Smaller firms need to spend more time working to be part of the selection process. If you're big, you probably shouldn't waste much time on these activities – in most cases buyers can't afford not to include you in a bid anyway. Thus, the stature of the supplier firm affects the NAM's ability to build trust through the transference process, and to acquire more sales as a result.

What we know about the routes to trust also suggests avenues for developing deep-rooted programs that can lock out the competition over the long run. Since risk is the requisite precursor to trust, this may require making your organization vulnerable to the customer – by sharing more strategic information, customizing products and services, or investing in strategic process improvements. Such investments, while risky, can tie the customer to you more closely. For example, making changes to the enterprise-wide buying process can take the cost out of the buying system for customers, often lowering costs without lowering price. This, however, requires a very intimate relationship with customers where sharing confidential data is the only way to make it happen. Clearly, the higher the stakes of the transaction, the more you have to lose.

However, the pay-off can be great if such investments create trust through the calculative or intentionality process.

The prediction process comes into play when designing the organization, simply by magnifying the old adage "time is money." The greatest investment a supplier firm can make in a customer is time—personal time. This can easily be calculated by the account load given to NAMs in the selling organization. A company that develops an account strategy that holds the accounts per NAM in the single digits is making a statement to the NAM and the customer concerning how much time they can and will spend with one another.

This is important because the ability to predict someone's behavior is directly correlated to how much opportunity you have to observe him or her. Observation provides a foundation for understanding and predicting behavior, and consequently, for building trust. Investments in social activities can be key to this strategy. These programs are often viewed as "boondoggle" type activities; however, the rewards can be enormous in facilitating the development of trust. The more time customers spend with NAMs in different environments, the more they feel confident in predicting a NAM's behavior in other situations. Something as simple as keeping score in a golf game can serve as a simple metaphor for behavior when the stakes are high in a buyer/seller relationship.

Further, social interactions can be leveraged to demonstrate a NAM's or supplier's capabilities (invoking the capability process) and sincere concern for the customer (intentionality process). Finally, if other people from the selling organization are included in social outings, trust might transfer to other members of the NAM's firm – institutionalizing the long-term relationship and broadening ownership of the relationship beyond the NAM alone.

Training Strategy

Training programs should take into account the skills needed to establish relationships with customers based on a high degree of trust. The capability process, which depends on the customer's assessment of the NAM's or supplier firm's ability to fulfill its promises, suggests several important areas for training. For example, companies might develop "promise training" programs. Such programs would include developing skills centered on processes that help NAMs be more responsive and consistent in their approach to customers (and keep their promises).

Trust may also be established via the capability process based on the NAM's expertise. Since customers trust NAMs who are experts, NAMs must master the technical skills necessary to convey expertise with respect to their products and industry. Certification programs are a great way to monitor and guarantee a certain level of expertise. In addition to effective internal training programs, external education should also be encouraged. Attending industry training programs with the buyer is the ultimate in trust-building activities for NAMs. And efficient, too – participation not only establishes credibility in the buyer's eyes, but also leads to competitive awareness.

While it is important for NAMs to establish their product and industry expertise, this may not be where NAMs stand to build a sustainable competitive advantage. Based on our knowledge of the capability process, we know that customers are more likely to trust NAMs who have the power to get things done. NAMs must navigate with ease within their own firms on behalf of the customer; however, many training programs focus exclusively on how to get at the top of the customer organization without any tools for the internal sell. The irony here is that even when NAMs can make contacts high in the customer organization, the advantage is short-lived unless they can demonstrate the ability to influence their own company's internal strategy and processes.

When NAMs are ill-equipped to effect change within their own company while managing expectations externally, the customer often perceives that the supplier firm is "inflexible." Therefore, to establish trust, we need to provide focus and skill building for NAMs on how to gain access to their own company's senior management and strategic planning process.

Strategy in Coaching Salespeople and Assigning People to Accounts

We all know that people do business with those they like or feel comfortable with. Although "likeability" is not often discussed in the sales coaching process or in the assignment of accounts, it is probably one of the most significant factors in developing trust between a buyer and a NAM. By being "likable," the best sales people establish a trusting relationship by stressing the commonalties between them and their customers, avoiding the differences, and working at "getting comfortable."

The fact that likeability leads to trust also has implications for the account assignment process. An interesting idea is to use individual customer profile information – on interests, hobbies, alma maters, etc. – to match NAMs with customers. In other words, use the amazing amount of personal information NAMs keep on their customers to match NAMs to customers who share common interests. This certainly gives the NAM and buyer a head start at building a trusting relationship. For example, trust can form more readily through the processes of prediction and intentionality when NAMs and buyers have the chance to see "eye to eye" on common non-work related interests. The best part, though, is that the common interest is not contrived – it is the result of effective "match making."

Compensation Strategy

In compensating NAMs, most companies start with transactions and then move to more "soft" measures as their NAM programs mature. Several surveys have revealed that as much as 50% of a NAM's performance compensation can be derived from non-revenue measures. Often, customer surveys are part of this evaluation. But what is interesting in examining many of these surveys is that the concept of trust is absent! Sometimes it shows up in the area of timeliness of response. However, if trust builds relationships, and relationships are a path to competitive advantage, shouldn't there be a trust index? Companies should know how their customers compare the levels of trust they have with their salespeople to those of their competitors' salespeople. It would be even better to identify what relationships customers perceive to have the highest level of trust operational—either in or out of the supplier's own industry. The key is learning what activities customers can identify that lead to this high level of trust.

The bottom line is that if a NAM compensation model includes customer surveys, there should be a focus on trust as the key driver of relationship assessments. Suggested areas to measure include:

- *Consistent performance:* Does the NAM provide consistent response and deliverables over time?

- *Expertise:* Is the NAM an expert? (Measures should go beyond product knowledge to include executive level skills for managing projects, information, and events.)

- *Information sharing:* Does the NAM create an atmosphere conducive to mutual disclosure?

- *Likeability:* Does the customer like the NAM? ("Likeability" may be best measured through third party questioning and informal interviewing.)

- *Ability to make change internally:* Does the customer think the NAM has the power to influence his/her own organization? (Although tricky to measure, this can raise red flags where customers are not connecting with NAMs because they are perceived to be ineffective in their own organization.)

Conclusion

As companies consider the trust-building processes outlined in this chapter, there are two keys to making the theory work. The first is understanding that customer relationships are essential in establishing a competitive foothold, and that trust is _the_ driving force behind building relationships. The second is that there are ways to link trust-building activities to sales behavior in order to reap a competitive advantage in the relationship building process. Simply put, being better than your best competitors at building trusting relationships could create the "stealth" competitive advantage that everyone is looking for.

CHAPTER X

Building Trust and Credibility One-On-One with the Customer

Gary Kunath
Principal
The Summit Group

CHAPTER X

Individual Trust: The Core Ingredient

Trust has become a primary focus in business relationships. The real challenge is how to build one-on-one trust with people in the account and how to do it quickly. This is the kind of trust that vaults your overall business relationship to the highest level with top decision makers, who can make a big difference in achieving sales targets.

Many training programs address ways to build trust and relationships with the customer. Many are insightful; however, many are complicated, theoretical, and not operational. The most powerful formula for building trust with individual customers is straightforward. The core of this formula is value generation.

The ability to generate value for customers and consistently impact their critical business issues is the single largest contributor to trust attainment in that business relationship. Even more potent is the ability to anticipate customer business problems and proactively address them with your best ideas and concepts. This will accelerate the depth of trust in a business relationship.

Personal relationships are also critical in the process of building trust. Demonstrated personal ethics, integrity, and overall individual demeanor are crucial in the trust-building process. No customer wants a business relationship with a sales person who behaves unethically, because someone with low ethical standards is incapable of bringing them any business value. The key ingredient is added value.

Trust in business relationships comes from value delivery and business impact. In fact, business impact transcends personal relationships in the decision making process. Many argue that having strong personal relationships afford certain advantages, but one simple rule still applies: the customers may love you, but they love themselves more!

Trust in the Business Relationship: The Ideal State

From a sales perspective, trust determines the depth of the overall business relationship with a customer, and this relationship determines attainment of sales quota. It is that simple.

Many sales people say that being considered a "Trusted Advisor" by their customers is the ultimate of business relationships (see Figure 1). They also want to achieve partnership or co-producer status with their best customers. This is not a simple task. What exactly does that mean, and more importantly, how is it achieved with key decision-makers?

Figure 1

CHARACTERISTICS OF A TRUSTED ADVISOR RELATIONSHIP
⇒ COLLABORATIVE, LONG-TERM RELATIONSHIP & JOINT RISK SHARING
⇒ BUSINESS PROCESSES ARE ALIGNED & INTEGRATED FOR BUSINESS SYNERGY
⇒ MULTIPLE LEVELS & FUNCTIONS, INCLUDING SENIOR EXECUTIVES, OF EACH ORGANIZATION ARE ACTIVELY INVOLVED IN THE RELATIONSHIP
⇒ YOU HAVE ACHIEVED "PART OF THE FAMILY" STATUS
⇒ HEAVY RELIANCE ON YOU TO HELP FORMULATE CUSTOMER PLANS & STRATEGIES
⇒ LOOKS TO YOU TO PROVIDE "THOUGHT LEADERSHIP" AND "BEST PRACTICE" CAPABILITY

These characteristics are not comprehensive, but they afford a perspective on this type of relationship. Clearly, a high level of trust exists within a Trusted Advisor relationship. The delivery of value (past, present, and future) is the key driver behind achieving this relationship status. The natural by-product of this type of relationship is more "share of customer," competitive immunity, higher margins, and stronger business-to-business relationships. This is what sales people strive for and what assures their long-term success.

Building Trust and Credibility with Executives

Account managers can build instant credibility and trust with key executives in their accounts. Executives trust people that have a track record of bringing them success. There is no substitute for consistent execution of value delivery when building trust with executives. The key issue is how to bring them success with no access and consequently no existing relationship. Also, many executives create barriers that are designed to prevent sales people from contacting them. This is because they have met too many sales people who cared only about pushing product versus value delivery. Executives want to spend their time meeting with sales people who have their interests at heart.

Executives are absolutely accessible, but there are very specific ground rules under which to gain access, establish instant credibility, and build trust. Executives evaluate your ability to contribute to their business within the first one to five minutes of your meeting with them. (See Figure 2 at the end of this chapter for a simple trust readiness test that you can use to determine if you are prepared to meet with executives and are able to build the foundation needed for gaining their trust. The more questions you can answer yes to will place you in a much stronger position to succeed in gaining access, building instant credibility, and attaining trust.)

The following contributions must be conveyed in the initial stages of contact in order to advance the relationship:

1. *Knowledge of customer business issues.* The depth of knowledge you have about customer business issues and your ability to express it in customer terms is crucial. Account managers need to know the business issues that keep these executives awake at night and have a comprehensive understanding of the key business processes that executives rely upon to drive value to their constituents. All businesses must manage the industry forces that affect their overall profitability. As a result of these forces, key business initiatives can be identified: Market/Brand initiatives, Strategic initiatives, Competitive initiatives, and Financial initiatives. Combined, these initiatives set the overall direction that the company will take to achieve profitability targets. This is called the "Customers' Compass." Strong understanding and articulation of the key business problems and corresponding customer initiatives will immediately differentiate the smart supplier from its competition.

2. *Dialogue content and questions.* The ability to align your business dialogue with the level and function of the executive you're a meeting is critical. It is imperative that you are cross-functionally and hierarchically competent. Engaging a vice president of customer care is very different than engaging a purchasing manager. Asking the right questions validates your business acumen in the mind of the executive. Appropriate questions for a VP of Customer Care may include: How is customer

satisfaction determined? How are these components identified, measured, prioritized and used for incentives? How do you identify repurchase intentions? How do you determine the customers' likely future market behavior? All of these go a long way toward establishing credibility, which is the precursor to trust.

3. *Quantity and depth of internal relations.* If you have strong internal relationships, it is critical that you share this with the executive in your opening conversation. Having strong relationships with people that these executives know and respect is invaluable in gaining their trust in a short cycle time. The best way to leverage these internal relationships is to have them contact the targeted executive prior to your visit. Fielding a call from someone they already know speeds up the trust process. Also, executives want to know that you have good relations throughout the organization because they won't have to sell you as hard within their own organization when they decide to make you a member of their team.

4. *Broad view of industry, competitors, and other industries.* One of the best ways to bring value to executives is to provide them with "Thought Leadership" and best practice capability in a very short cycle time. If you can accelerate their migration down the learning curve, you will have gone a long way in attaining their trust.

5. *Willingness to absorb all or partial risk.* One of the best ways to build trust quickly with an executive is to proactively provide options to eliminate or reduce their risk in key initiatives and value delivery options. The value delivery options you propose to targeted executives must

contain a high degree of certainty that they will be realized. Reducing risk signals that you know risk is important to them and that you have looked at the business situation from their perspective. It also demonstrates a high degree of confidence in the approach being offered. Fast prototyping, cash flow options, guarantees/warranties, financing/funding options, taking payment as a percentage of the proposed value delivery, and revenue or expense sharing are some of the key items that are used to build instant credibility and trust.

6. *Quality of business solutions.* Your approach to problem solving is important in building trust. Your knowledge of customer business problems and your best ideas that directly impact those problems are key. You must incorporate into your initial conversation a compelling reason for them to listen to you. This 'value statement' is your key to establishing instant credibility and positioning for long-term trust. It is not necessary to have all of the metrics or quantify the exact level of business impact. If you can provide successful examples in related companies with similar problems where your approach has worked, you are in a strong position to advance the relationship.

7. *Professional background, titles, achievements, and training.* The degree of impact these things have on an executive varies from person to person. In the early stages of developing the relationship, this can afford you a strong foundation for gaining entry and may even grant you a second chance if needed.

8. *Mutual backgrounds, common relationships and affiliations.* Most executives are involved in numerous community and so-

cial activities. This is one of the best venues in which to establish initial contact with executives. If you both have similar backgrounds, relationship, or affiliations, it will provide the executive with insights about you that a sales meeting would never afford. Affiliations describe you and your priorities and are a common bond. Should you have such alignments with a targeted executive, mentioning them early can take your relationship to a much stronger level much more quickly, thereby building trust.

Conclusions

The most effective way to gain access to key executives and build instant credibility and trust on an individual basis is through value delivery. In short, you must deliver the value you have promised your customer. When building trust with key executives, how you articulate your abilities and convince them that you have the capacity to truly move their business is crucial.

Figure 2

TRUST READINESS TEST FOR EXECUTIVE RELATIONSHIPS

The purpose of this test is to allow you to check the level of your business readiness to actually meet with senior executives within your customers' organization and will serve as a determinant of your ability to gain instant credibility and trust, one on one. You must be able to bring them value that impacts factors within their business that keep them awake at night. This test features business knowledge questions that should serve as check points for you that will be instrumental in gaining access to the top executives and will help ensure that the content quality of your dialogue, once in, increases your chances for success to build a relationship with high trust. If you can comfortably discuss and/ or answer any of the questions listed below, in direct customer terms, then there isn't an executive alive who won't meet with you and gain value from that meeting. These are issues that executives want you to be able to discuss before they will ever consider you as a trusted advisor and allow you entry.

YOU ARE PREPARED TO MEET WITH THE EXECUTIVE IF YOU CAN ANSWER THESE QUESTIONS:		Yes	No
1. Do you know the top business issues that keep this executive awake at night?			
2. Do you have a comprehensive understanding of the key business processes that this executive relies upon to drive value?			
3. Can you articulate the value differentiators that this executive considers vital to his/ her customer top business initiatives?			
4. Do you have profound knowledge of the key business initiatives / metrics within each of the Customer Compass categories as they apply to this executive? (i.e. Strategic Direction, Financial Re-Engineering, Brand Management, Competitiveness)			

THE MEETING WILL BE OF HIGH VALUE TO THE EXECUTIVE IF YOU CAN DISCUSS ONE OR MORE OF THESE QUESTIONS:		Yes	No
5a. Can you articulate how you can use any or all of your total company resources / offer enablers to impact key business initiatives that this executive relies upon to generate value? Can you articulate this impact in customer terms that are meaningful to this executive?			
5b. Can you provide this executive with the level to which you might be able to impact these business initiatives and provide compelling proof to support your position? Can you help this executive gather compelling proof to support moving forward with you and / or help identify and build support with key players in the customer organization?			
6. Are you prepared to present a variety of business options available to this executive even if some of those options do not directly involve you?			
7. Can you supply this executive with market intelligence on industry trends, competitive initiatives or best practices inside or outside his/her industry that benefits their business position?			
8. Can you supply "Thought Leadership" to this executive? 8a. Can you reduce cycle time for this executive relative to goal attainment?			
9. Do you know the barriers, risks or any other constraints this executive is faced with and can you discuss appropriate courses of action?			
10. Can you demonstrate previous experience and past successes within this executives' industry or with other organizations experiencing similar problems, issues or opportunities?			

CHAPTER XI

The Impact of Organizational Alignment on Trust

Doug Bosse
Senior Consultant
S4 Consulting

Joe Sperry
Partner
S4 Consulting

CHAPTER XI

In customer-supplier relationships, reliability is a key component of trust. Making organizations reliable, though, requires systematic programs and processes. It's a painful irony: the programs and processes which offer suppliers the greatest opportunity for sustainable differentiation are exactly those processes and programs which are hardest to implement. Were implementation easy, suppliers would already have done it. Value-added strategic account management—which can offer significant supplier differentiation—can be explained in five minutes. But in most cultures, true strategic account management *cannot* be executed: over fifty per cent of all strategic account management programs fail to hit their first year objectives, and of those firms that *do* hit their first year goals, a significantly high percentage fail to meet their second year goals.

We argue that one of the primary difficulties in implementing value-added strategic account management is that, in most cases, implementation requires a fundamental examination and re-design of the supplier organization. To consistently exceed a strategic account's expectations, the supplier *must* create a trusting relationship with the account; to create trust, the supplier organization *must* speak with one voice. To speak with one voice, though, requires the supplier to overcome the driving internal logic of each of its functions. In most cases, this means the supplier must overcome the very goals, objectives and compensation systems it has created for departments such as production, shipping, accounting, MIS and all the rest. The vast majority of these objectives drive employees to increase the efficiency and effectiveness of internal processing—**not** to exceed strategic account expectations. If the supplier does not align the goals, objectives and compensation systems of each function interacting with the strategic account, trust becomes a wish rather than an integral part of the supplier's strategic account relationship management. As a result, cases such as those presented below will occur again and again:

Case Study #1:

A huge manufacturer's largest national account was having cash flow problems. The manufacturer's Strategic Account Manager and the Marketing Department were working furiously to help the account, but no one mentioned this effort to the past due accounts receivable clerk. And so, at sixty days, this accounting clerk did what he was paid to do: cut off all product delivery and send one of those dunning letters that seem to suggest the passing of debtors' prison was not really a major step forward for civilization. The national account, furious, sent a check for all moneys owed and never did business with the supplier again. Over half the manufacturers we work with or train cringe when we tell this story. Most of them have a similar story.

Case Study #2:

A high-tech service firm was radically downsizing and putting pressure on all remaining personnel to generate incremental revenue. The accounting department decided to examine the invoices sent to the supplier's largest accounts over the last ten years, found numerous errors, and then sent "corrected" invoices--without mentioning any of this to the supplier's strategic account managers. We were interviewing an Executive VP at one of the supplier's strategic accounts, who furiously called the process "forensic accounting." The supplier ended up disciplining the Accounting Manager for following his own directives (reasoning that someone had to take the blame). The damage to the strategic account relationship, though, had already been done.

Case Study #3:

A final example, this time from an executive strategic account contact interview: "A year ago we signed a contract to build a distribution system between our two companies. The contract clearly stated that we would be running product from other suppliers through that channel. The week the product was supposed to start flowing, (the supplier's) materials person said they would be charging us $18,000 per year as an affiliation fee. We didn't hear this from our rep but from this other employee who was looking only at his responsibility. I told him about our contract and he said it was meaningless to him. Our rep then said she couldn't influence the materials person. She told us to pay the fee for two months while she tried to straighten it out. I won't do that."

Lessons Learned

An inescapable prerequisite of trust in a strategic account relationship is the supplier's ability to make *organizational* rather than individual or departmental promises. If a supplier commitment is known and acted upon by only a handful of people in one department—usually Sales/Marketing—for all practical purposes, no real commitment has been made by the organization. And those promises, no matter who makes them, will likely be broken. As Dave Packard, co-founder of Hewlett-Packard, once said, "Marketing is far too important to be left to the Marketing Department."

When we look at those organizations that have managed to implement true value-added strategic account relationship management, we tend to see two things: 1) selecting the right people to manage strategic relationships, and 2) providing the infrastructure that allows those individuals to manage strategic relationships. This infrastructure usually includes clear strategic marketing goals, clear objectives for the Strategic Account Management process, cross-functional teams to overcome supplier internal focus and inertia, high levels of executive support, and a networked real-time computer system by which all supplier functions can monitor and manage those relationships deemed "strategic." Without the supporting infrastructure and the means to coordinate communication with which to live up to commitments, the supplier will not be able to deliver true added value to its strategic accounts. Equally as bad, the account manager can become a glorified sales or service person, instead of a strategic relationship owner.

In suppliers that have not developed this account management infrastructure, some strategic account managers are still able to accomplish great things. Some of these account managers, gifted influencers with carefully nurtured pre-existing internal relationships, have been able to make and then deliver on organizational promises—but only for a time, and at great cost to the supplier. The absence of infrastructure means that the strategic account manager has to spend more time managing internal than external relationships. This is not the way to optimize the strategic account manager's value to either the supplier or the strategic account. The strategic account manager, however gifted and dedicated, cannot manage *all* supplier/strategic account interactions all the time. Sooner or later there will be unreliability, inconsistency, miscommunication and a lessening of trust. Given enough unreliability, the strategic relationship will end.

Over the last ten years we have conducted over 600 interviews with lost strategic accounts. In over 80% of the interviews, account contacts said they stopped doing business with their supplier because they felt "badly treated." When we tried to define what is meant by "badly treated," the answer was "suppliers that have not lived up to commitments and organizational promises". The contacts at the strategic account note the poor performance, feel deceived, complain, and then switch suppliers when their complaints do not lead to improved supplier performance.

Tom Peters once argued that the true job of the CEO is to "get everyone headed in roughly the same direction." We believe that this is also the true job of suppliers serving strategic accounts. Unless those firms align their functions' goals, objectives and compensation systems, different departments will be sending very different marketing messages to the strategic accounts. And if accounts perceive they are receiving individual rather than organizational commitments, developing trust—a pre-requisite for developing value-added strategic account relationships—becomes an impossibility for the supplier and a golden opportunity for a savvy competitor.

CHAPTER XII:

How Trust Leads to Success

Gerhard Gschwandtner
Publisher
Selling Power Magazine

CHAPTER XII

How many people do you trust at work? All of them, or only a few? In a survey of 1,324 randomly selected workers, managers and executives in a variety of industries, 48% of the respondents admit to taking unethical or illegal actions in the past year. The survey was sponsored by the Ethics Officer Association and the American Society of Chartered Life Underwriters & Chartered Financial Consultants. The 236-page study asked workers to list only violations that were caused by work pressures such as sales quotas, long hours, job insecurity or personal challenges related to work. The survey did not list violations due to internal pressures such as greed, anger or envy. The study also indicates that things are getting worse. A significant 57% say that they feel more pressure to be unethical today than they did five years ago, while 40% say that the situation has worsened over the last year. In reference to the survey, USA TODAY wrote, "violations are so rampant that if you aren't stealing company property, leaking company secrets or lying to customers and supervisors, the odds are the worker next to you is."

Although companies often take great pains to develop a code of ethics, the subject of building trust is rarely mentioned in the top executive suite. While a code of ethics specifies what people should not do, the creation of trust depends on what people actually do. Trust is an intangible yet critical asset in any corporation. Paradoxically, it does not get measured until it is lost. Unlike other assets, trust can't be purchased on the market; it has to be earned over a long period of time and it must be carefully nurtured. If we fail to nurture trust, it will disappear overnight.

Mistrust is a Fact of Life

Extensive research shows that employees mistrust their company, companies mistrust their employees, and customers mistrust salespeople and vendor companies. Every industry has its own unique problems with trustworthiness. The pharmaceutical industry is victimized by unethical drug manufacturers that fraudulently reproduce expensive brand-name drugs and sell them wholesale to unethical pharmacists. The securities industry is infected by unethical salespeople who promise their customers unrealistic gains while selling nearly worthless financial products. Distrust of health care providers has been on the rise for years with reports of overcharging and mismanagement. Even charitable foundations have come into the spotlight due to managers who betrayed the trust of generous donors by lining their own pockets.

The computer industry is filled with ethical violations. *Computerworld* magazine recently conducted an anonymous survey of 255 IS professionals in which nearly half (47%) of the respondents admitted to copying commercial software without authorization. Yet 78% of all respondents agreed that it should never be done. One IS manager stated, "The company hired me three months ago. When I turned my attention to software inventory, I discovered hundreds of illegal copies and very few licenses. I took the issue to the president of the company and was told I was hired to save money and not to cost them money."

The cause of mistrust often boils down to a human error in judgment. In computer software sales, the ignorance of a client is often seen as an invitation for exploitation. For example, system developers often fail to give their customers an objective appraisal of the true difficulties of a project, or overstate the economic value of the final product. As a result, customers often pour money into software projects that are doomed to fail from the beginning.

To understand the importance of trust, one has to assess the damage caused by people who don't see the benefits of trustworthiness. While betrayal of trust enrages us, the actions of untrustworthy employees end up costing billions of dollars. Guardsmark, an employee screening company, estimates the cost of employee theft at about $120 billion a year. According to a survey by publisher McGraw-Hill/London House, entry-level fast food employees steal $239 a year in cash and merchandise. However, employees don't have a monopoly on betrayal of trust. The business press is filled with examples of corporate wrongdoing. Just last year dozens of CEOs of well-known companies swallowed hard, admitting no guilt, but at the same time paid huge settlements to make good for ethical violations.

Mistrust is a widely accepted social affliction that affects all professions. The most recent Gallup poll on public trust shows that we don't trust anyone 100%. Americans give the military a 64% trust rating, the police earned only 58% and religion is in third place with a 57% trust factor. Among the professions, the highest trust ratings went to 1) pharmacists, 2) individual clergy, 3) doctors, 4) dentists, 5) engineers and 6) college professors. The survey also revealed that clergy are trusted more than twice as much as journalists – who, in turn, are twice as trusted as lawmakers. It is ironic that every one of us expects others to be trustworthy, but we rarely conduct a reality check on our own trustworthiness.

Trust is Everyone's Business
Stephen Covey, author of *The Seven Habits of Highly Effective People*, says trust has to be earned, and the only way to earn

it is to become actively trustworthy. With all the talk about value-added selling, people overlook the fact that the highest values of companies reside in the hearts of their people. The inherent values of honesty, integrity and courage all hinge on the common virtue of trustworthiness. Trustworthiness is the backbone of good management. The trend toward globalization of all businesses requires more cooperation in a climate of mutual trust. While distrust creates disconnects, developing trustworthiness can build economic power. In an interview with *Industry Week*, Frank Sonnenberg, author of *Managing With a Conscience* (McGraw-Hill, 1994), stated, "Where they were once self-sufficient, companies will become increasingly dependent on strategic alliances, supplier relationships, and even contract employees to support their lean staffs. In the past, conventional wisdom dictated playing one supplier against another, spending endless hours in the negotiating process, and then calculating ways to gain an upper hand. Managing with a conscience means understanding that our destinies are closely intertwined with our partners. We must kill the 'we/they' mentality and replace it with a new "us" mentality that allows everyone to reach their full potential."

Why We Ignore Trustworthiness

The drive to be number one often leads to a domino effect where trustworthiness tumbles. Many industry leaders flaunt their ambition by bragging that "total world domination" is their corporate mission. For everyone who disapproves of Microsoft's not-so-secret monopolistic objectives, there are millions who would like to control the world market like Bill Gates does. What do Bill Gates wannabes do? They lead their salespeople with blind ambition.

The primary focus of blind ambition is to reach out for immediate, selfish gains and to block out any injury to trust. Salespeople who operate in a corporate culture consumed by blind ambition often feel pressured to oversell their clients in the hopes of improving the bottom line for the quarter. Once the numbers are reached, the company proudly displays the new sales record while its customers quietly forge new relationships with more trustworthy companies. In the race for world dominance, hunting companies often turn into passionately hunted organizations. It is no wonder that *Fortune 500* companies rarely last more than 25 years. The lesson that CEOs could learn by examining the causes of business failures? Greed is the seed merchant of distrust.

Trust is a Matter of 360 Degrees

Creating trust is not the same intellectual challenge as finding a new angle for getting more business. Trust demands that heart, mind and soul are engaged and invested in the circle of business that involves all relationships, internal and external. Trustworthiness is equally important to everyone: the employee, the manager, the supplier, the customer, the stockholder and the community at large. Trust is not a question of being nice from nine to five; it demands vigilance around the clock. Trust isn't about what we do on American soil, under American law; it's about what we do around the globe. Trust isn't what we say when someone is listening; trust depends on what we do when nobody is watching. Trust is a matter of 360 degrees—no more, no less. Trust doesn't subdivide; it is an all-or-nothing proposition. If one stakeholder betrays the circle of trust created by a group of people, everyone suffers.

How To Build Trust

Effective leaders can build trust by encouraging people to rally behind an idea dedicated to the common good. When President Harry Truman declared, "the buck stops here," he sent a powerful message indicating that he took responsibility for the trustworthiness of his administration. William Holland, chairman and CEO of United Dominion Industries (Charlotte, NC) once wrote, "In my opinion, there is one basic policy that tolerates no exceptions: play it straight with the public, stockholders, customers, suppliers, employees, or any other individual or group. The only right way to deal with people is forthrightly and honestly. If mistakes are made, admit them right away and correct them as soon as possible."

Trustworthiness in an organization is not a matter of printing a code of ethics and publishing a handbook for employees. More important is creating an atmosphere in which employees feel free to admit mistakes and discuss ethical questions without fear of hurting their careers. Richard Harrison, VP of Sales for IBM, recently told *Selling Power* magazine that he creates an "amnesty environment" in sales meetings where salespeople can talk freely about their difficulties with the company or their customers. Open communication is one of the best builders of trust and confidence. Leaders who encourage continual debate can advance trust while encouraging people to hold themselves to higher standards. Without an open exchange of thoughts and feelings, people tend to become isolated and narrow-minded individuals. While ongoing communication is vital to maintaining trustworthiness, every employee from the top executive to the janitor has to "walk the talk".

When Stanley Gault became Chairman and CEO of Goodyear, he established trust within the first week with a series of simple steps. He brought his own postage stamps to the office. He started an open-door policy that he adhered to strictly. He took phone calls from Goodyear customers, listened to their complaints and resolved them on the spot. Within a year, Gault achieved an amazing turnaround in morale, sales and profits. Herb Kelleher, Chairman of Southwest Airlines, created an organization that has become a role model for the airline industry. Kelleher built trust in the customer by focusing on the company's most valuable resource: its employees. Says Kelleher, "If you really want to put the customer first, then you have to put the employee more first." Only the employee who is turned on is going to create a fabulous experience for the customer. Kelleher walks the talk. He is a hands-on, roll-up-the-sleeves executive who tries to keep things simple. He once arm-wrestled a CEO to avoid a costly legal dispute. He lost the case, but his credibility continues to soar.

Trust At Every Step of the Sale

How can we create an atmosphere of trust in a sales organization? Trustworthy salespeople establish long-lasting relationships with customers. Establishing trust with a customer is like creating an invisible bank account. With each successful sale, we make a deposit that is held in a special trust account. With each good deed - like when we help our customer solve a problem - we add to our deposit and over time we are allowed to make withdrawals in the form of favors. With each problem we create for the customer – like when our delivery is late – we run the risk of losing the customer's trust. A single mistake can wipe out all deposits we have made over a long period of time.

Here are twelve key ideas designed to build trust within a sales organization:

1. Have a "field of dreams" approach to life. If you build trust, people will come to you. If you lose trust, people will leave you.

2. Create a customer, not a sale. The investment in a better relationship with a customer costs fewer dollars than the investment in finding and creating a new customer.

3. Every relationship advances through "moments of trust." Moments of trust are not created by promises, but by action. If you are a sales manager, the way you respond to someone who brings you bad news will determine how much information people will bring to you in the future.

4. Monitor your own trustworthiness just as much as you expect others to be trustworthy.

5. Trust demands vigilance. Little things make the difference. Return all phone calls, faxes and e-mails on time. Send thank-you notes. Remember birthdays.

6. Deliver proof even if nobody asks for it. When you make a significant claim in your sales presentation, automatically offer the supporting backup document.

7. Walk the talk. Communicators often create the perception of trustworthiness by manipulating their body language. If you try to fake trust, you'll lose trust forever.

8. Trust involves the brain and the heart. Stephen Covey says, "you can buy a person's hand, but you can't buy his heart." You can only earn the trust of your team if you respect and trust each team member.

9. Show compassion. Salespeople who have compassion for other people's needs, feelings, and dreams are perceived as more trustworthy. Self-centered managers tend to be insensitive and often lose the trust of their employees.

10. Be aware that power can contaminate trust. Too much power and too little power tend to create distrust. People in power have an obligation to treat all people with the same respect and dignity.

11. Communicate clearly. Professional communicators craft concise messages. They avoid convoluted messages. They practice simplicity. They are patient educators. Salespeople who remove complexity and bring clarity to the relationship earn more trust.

12. Create a hierarchy where no position is superior to another. True empowerment means abandoning the idea that the manager decides and the employee abides. Empowered employees recognize only one ruling dictator—customer satisfaction.

EPILOGUE

The Trust Imperative

Roger Dow
Vice President, General Sales Manager
Marriott Lodging

ENTHUSED
CUSTOMERS

INSPIRED
PEOPLE

FINANCIAL
PERFORMANCE

TRUSTING
RELATIONSHIPS

8. Lead With Care

7. Unleash the Power of People

6. Measure Well, Act Fast

5. Make Technology Your Servant

4. Simplify, Simplify, Simplify

3. Have the Courage to Set Bold Goals

2. Make Every Customer Feel Special

1. Build a Strong Foundation

The Trust-Based Organization

EPILOGUE

The Beginnings

In our book, *TURNED ON—Eight Vital Insights to Energize Your People, Customers, and Profits,* Sue Cook and I describe a proven business model for achieving long-term vitality. We spent two years researching extraordinarily successful organizations with the goal of identifying any practices they might have in common that differentiated them from their far less successful competitors. From our learnings, we distilled **Eight Vital Insights** that these companies used as the essential building blocks to achieve success.

While these companies are among America's most admired, each of them labeled itself a "work in progress" and admitted it didn't have all the answers. Another trait they share is their pursuit of long-term vitality guided by an equal obsession with: *Energized People, Enthusiastic Customers,* and *Financial Performance.*

The Trust Imperative—Our Model Evolves

Our research for this book caused Lisa Napolitano, Mike Pusateri, and me to *peel back the onion* in order to understand the role "trust" and "trusting relationships" play in enabling NAMs and their organizations to accelerate growth and achieve their strategic objectives. In the preceding chapters, the contributing academics, consultants, publisher, and business leaders all agree that "trust" and "trusting relationships" are critical to transitioning to the *new way of doing business,* which is evolving in the face of today's fiercely competitive global markets.

After exploring the subject for the past year, it has become very clear to my colleagues and me that "trust" or "lack of trust" can have a profound impact on a company's ability to create competitive advantage and build share with its *high potential* customers. My greatest fear is that too many organizations will continue to give trust *lip service*—after all, who doesn't talk positively about trust—and not make building trust an uncompromising, integral part of their business strategy. When we asked the people involved in the compelling case studies if they could have achieved similar results without firmly establishing trust between all parties, the answer was a resounding "Absolutely not!"

Based on this **"trust imperative"**, I am compelled to add *Trusting Relationships* as a necessary core element to our business model. When we wrote *TURNED ON*, we made the following observations about the essence of long-term vitality:

> "The true face of long-term vitality might surprise you -- *the future of business lies in the ability to use modern capabilities to recapture the personal relationships of times past.* "

> "When companies were smaller and less complex, there existed a healthy balance between making money and doing what was right for people and customers. Personal relationships, tailored products, and hand-crafted service were the rule."

> "...The organizations in this book use modern capabilities to return full circle to *personal* products, services, and relationships. In striking a balance among people, customers, and profits, they rekindle a feeling of comfort and rightness that we all intuitively cherish."

These words very accurately describe a major change that is taking place between customer and supplier organizations, fueled by enlightened leaders and NAMs. As our contributors rightly point out and support with their case studies, a *new way of doing business* is evolving where "interdependent trusting relationships" are redefining business processes and taking traditional customer/supplier relationships to advanced levels. The result is a clear "win - win - WIN", where both the customer and supplier organizations mutually benefit, moving beyond their old transaction-oriented adversarial relationship, by focusing on creating a true WIN for the ultimate consumer. Therefore, the business model for the successful trust-based organization has evolved to strike a balance among Inspired *People, Enthusiastic Customers, Financial Performance,* and *Trusting Relationships.*

Once They've Seen The Light...

This book began with Jordan Lewis musing on what UFO aliens might think after observing how little trust exists between buyer and seller companies here on earth. He prophetically hypothesized that their only possible conclusion would be: "They must be crazy!" He quickly ticked off five clear examples of how trust between buyer and seller became the cornerstone for achieving extraordinary results that exponentially exceeded anything dreamed possible with the traditional low-trust transactional paradigm.

One would think that results like: *completed in record time with a $75 million cost savings...consistently the most profitable retailer in the world...the lowest per vehicle cost in the industry...purchasing costs dropping three times faster...cut construction time from 180 days to 22...* would result in every CEO in the world scrambling to find out how their company can get in on the action. Yet, the list is small, but growing, of companies that truly understand the potential opportunities and are willing to invest the time/effort/resources, endure the organizational pain, and make the top to bottom commitment which we've learned is necessary to succeed.

We observed that some organizations, intuitively believing there *had to be a better way*, explored the vision of building mutually beneficial trust-based customer/supplier relationships as the way to take their already successful companies to a new level of competitive advantage, while times were good. Among these examples are: Britain's Marks & Spencer, Motorola, Proctor & Gamble, Wal-Mart, and Bose. Other organizations, like Hewlett-Packard and Chrysler, chose this route when their historical ways of doing business produced diminishing returns, and when the industrial landscape that they knew so well had changed dramatically. For them, it wasn't about a compelling new vision—it was about survival.

No matter what led them down the road of creating trust-based customer/supplier relationships to achieve the common goal of delighting the end consumer, their future direction and business strategy is forever changed. When they see the rest of the world continuing to pound away at low-trust/transactional relationships, they too conclude, "They must be crazy!" Although they all agree that the process is extremely difficult, once they've seen the light they can't imagine going back to their former adversarial selling rituals.

Now What—Does Anyone Have a Road Map?

Perhaps you're feeling like me at this point -- this book has been a little like drinking from a fire hose. Our contributors have kindly shared a wealth of information, observations, cautions, lessons learned, hands-on experience, recommendations, and advice. I am impressed by what some organizations are doing, excited about the possibilities, and (I'll admit it...) a bit intimidated by the awesome organizational commitment that successfully implementing the "trust imperative" will take. However, I've had the pleasure of spending time with our book's collaborators. While they may have an insight or two and a little head start, they are sales, purchasing, and business people like you and me—so it isn't impossible.

If you've been around the block a few times, like me, I think you'll agree that we intuitively know in our gut that this is the only way to go if we are to ensure long-term vitality. Every success or failure we've experienced in trying to build vibrant and growing personal and organizational relationships reaffirms the insights on the preceding pages. We now have the challenge of pulling together all that has been said into a cohesive plan that we can begin to implement with our *high potential* customers and suppliers.

With advance apology to our collaborators for their wisdom that I unintentionally did not include, the following is an overview of how we might integrate their knowledge and experience into our business strategy using the **Eight Vital Insights** for building a trust-based organization.

1. Build a Strong Foundation

The most consistent advice we heard was to take the time up front to build a strong foundation. It will become the framework to support your efforts -- if the fundamentals aren't right, nothing else will be. It is important to understand that asking people to embrace trust-based relationships may be contrary to what is going on around them. In **Chapter XII**, Gerhard Gschwandtner provided a reality check with the statistics that *48% of surveyed business people* *admit to taking illegal or unethical actions in the past year* which they said were *caused by work pressures.* Unfortunately, things are getting worse -- *57% feel more pressure to be unethical than five years ago...mistrust is a widely accepted social affliction that afflicts all professions.*

NAMs can be more successful by understanding that trust is a continuum where customers go through various *processes* to evaluate the trustworthiness of their NAM, and more important, the organization the NAM represents. These processes are well defined in **Chapters III and IX**. The important learning here is that sellers tend to put more emphasis on building trust through a *relational process,* which is based on the emotional aspects of their personal relationships. However, buyers put their stock in a *transactional process,* which is driven by economic forces, rules, and penalties. Once we understand that trust can be built using five different processes, we can build a strong foundation of trust with our customers by combining these processes. The processes that have the most impact on trust are based on proven capabilities, past history, and a quantifiable cost/benefit ratio.

There are several critical areas on which to focus in building the strong foundation for transitioning from traditional transaction-based relationships to trust-based relationships:

⇒ It is important to align activities of both organizations beyond just selling and buying. Special attention should be paid to management, decision-making, location, structure, culture, politics, and priorities. The goal is to find a way to adjust to each other's way of doing business. Most efforts fail when these areas are not adequately addressed in advance.

⇒ The level of trust required increases proportionately with the complexity of the interaction, importance of the relationship, and level of risk involved.

⇒ In-depth knowledge of products and services is much more important than sales ability. Providing training on products and services will yield greater benefit than sales technique training. **Chapter X** provides excellent insight on how building knowledge of the industry and competitors will increase the NAMs value to client senior executives by positioning them as a "thought leader" and "best practice" provider.

⇒ As stated in **Chapter XI**, reliability to consistently implement processes that provide the greatest value to the customer is seen as very important. With so many different functional areas interacting with the customer, this is very hard to do, and even harder to sustain without organizational change. Success will be limited if the organization is not able to make fundamental changes in its business processes.

⇒ Market-based research conducted by A.T. Kearney (**Chapter IV**), concludes that there is an "expectations gap" between what retailers and manufacturers value and what each believes is important to the other. It turns out that they both place high value on the same things in a relationship, i.e. the need to be understood, openness, partnership, honesty, trust, and "speak my language". The paradox is that neither believes that these "softer side" variables are important to the other—but they are.

⇒ **Chapter IV** emphasizes the importance of both organizations sharing a common end-to-end vision and the same goals for the relationship. The vision and goals must be seen as part of a "grand plan" that mutually benefits both parties, improves their competitiveness, and is directed to the benefit of the end consumer.

⇒ When considering the "grand plan", don't set your sights too low. Keep in mind the JIT II case study (**Chapter VI**). This is probably the ultimate customer/supplier relationship, with vendor personnel working in the Bose plant and placing orders on themselves using Bose purchase orders.

⇒ We learned from Chrysler in **Chapter VIII** that a major key to any organization's future success is the strength of its supply base and how the supply chain continues to push the envelope of current practices.

2. Make Every Customer Feel Special
All NAMs certainly know what it takes to make their customers feel special. When you apply this insight to a trust-based relationship, it takes on new meaning. It requires moving beyond personal interaction in the business and social setting. The key findings we learned from trust-based relationships were:

⇒ Customers' needs have to be understood beyond the NAM at all levels of the organization that interact with the customer. The NAM must communicate these needs and get the commitment of everyone involved to make meeting those needs a top priority.

⇒ Both companies must understand, accept, and respect the other's value system. The importance of taking the time to learn a lot about each other is stressed in **Chapter V**. *Culture compatibility* is essential—and Hewlett-Packard cautions that sometimes there is not a fit, which makes building a trust-based partnership much more difficult, if not impossible.

⇒ In **Chapter IX**, we learn that the 80 / 20 rule may not be true. Many NAMs are finding they are getting more of their business from an even *smaller* percentage of customers. It is not uncommon for the number of customers covered by a NAM to be in the single digits, which makes these customers very important strategically. The role of the NAM, in these instances, is shifting to spending less time selling and devoting more time to understanding and communicating needs, gaining acceptance of ideas, and tailoring products and services to meet customers' current and future needs.

⇒ With NAMs spending more time with their customers, it is important that there is a good personality fit between them. Research indicates that "likeability" can be a factor in building trust. Look for common interests -- customer personal profiles should be taken into account when assigning NAMs. In **Chapter X**, Gary Kunath builds a case for considering mutual backgrounds, common relationships, and affiliations of client senior executives.

⇒ Kunath states that customer trust of the NAM and its organization is directly tied to "value generating" ability. He defines this as finding what keeps your customers up at night, knowing their business issues, identifying their key problems and initiatives, and becoming a "trusted advisor" on these areas. To evaluate where you stand in this regard with your customers and identify areas to work on, we recommend taking the **Trust Readiness Test for Executives** in **Chapter X**.

⇒ A mutual commitment to confidentiality is essential for any trust-based partnership to develop beyond the "product provider" level. It takes a major leap of faith for companies to share proprietary information, especially when they know that suppliers may potentially do business with their competitors. When confidential information is shared, the relationship moves to a new level. This results in reduced cycle time and more joint problem solving. The sharing of confidential information signals that you are considered part of the *family* and accelerates the trust building process.

⇒ Customers involved in high trust relationships expect to be treated *specially*, as if their relationship was *truly valued* at every level of the supplier organization. Yet, in over 600 interviews with *lost* strategic accounts, S4 Consulting (**Chapter XI**) was told by the account contact that they stopped doing business with their supplier, because they felt "badly treated". Suppliers had not lived up to their organizational promises…"*they lied to us!*" The trust that may have taken years to build was broken. The strategically important customer no longer felt *special* and moved to a new supplier.

3. Have the Courage to Set Bold Goals

The organizations in the case studies set bold goals to change the way they do business and their extraordinary results speak for themselves. As Jerome Lewis stated, over 50% of a firm's revenue goes to suppliers. This is too substantial a number to not be boldly addressed with respect to reducing the cost or getting more for the money being spent. The only way to effectively do this is to work creatively with suppliers toward a common goal, joining ideas and energy, and sharing (as partners) in the upside results.

Companies dedicated to pursuing this *new way of doing business* are dedicated to an emerging business model where relationships are considered as strategic assets that need to be invested in, according to the A. T. Kearney study. These *advanced relationships* require the creation of "multi-enterprise alliances" that span the entire supply chain from raw materials to distribution to the ultimate consumer. John Neuman predicts that the organizations that don't aggressively move to this model will ultimately be unable to compete and will perish. Those who are able to do it will become the future *category dominators*, enjoying greatly enhanced customer satisfaction, share growth, and profits. The evidence is mounting that this view is correct:

⇒   Chrysler believes that the future is about creating *totally linked supply chains*, where trust is a critical component in the equation. The high level of trust and partnership between Chrysler and its suppliers has resulted in the lowest comparable per vehicle cost in the automotive industry. Chrysler appropriately calls this the Extended Enterprise™. This model "moves participants to compete, not just as individual enterprises, but as *complete supply chains*," according to Dave Pearce.

⇒ Bose has taken the trusted-partner concept even further with its suppliers. They actually work in the Bose plant and are considered as part of the team, right down to their Bose nametags. Suppliers are involved *early* at the point of product design. In addition to the purchasing efficiencies, Bose gets the benefit of their product knowledge, ideas for reducing costs, and reduced cycle time. The supplier enjoys preferred supplier status and has the opportunity to *design-in* their product at the concept stage.

⇒ It is critical to agree upon the criteria and objectives for the partnership right up front and understand the level of investment it will require. P & G told us that this is mandatory, or you risk wasting a lot of time and resources. You can't get a return on investment without making the investment.

⇒ Hewlett-Packard found that not all customers are candidates for their stated goal of becoming their customer's "trusted-advisor". This takes a great deal of openness and commitment from both parties. Some customers are not suited or not interested in this level of involvement. The challenge is hard enough, without compromising success by choosing the wrong partner. HP doesn't have the time, energy, or resources to be a "trusted-advisor" to every customer. Therefore, they have three levels of customer involvement. Trust is important at every level, but it becomes more important as the complexity of the level increases.

By their very nature, these bold initiatives usually mandate organizational change and modification of the recognition and reward systems. Having worked with many companies on building trust-based alliances, Doug Bosse concludes that the consistent ability to implement true value-added alliances requires organizational redesign. High levels of cooperation won't happen without both organizations being able to speak to each other with *one voice*. This is the key to overcoming the sometimes-immovable *internal logic* of each internal function within a company that will thwart and wear down bold attempts to build value-added alliances. The internal reward, recognition, and objectives are often at "cross purposes" with the alliance effort. Guess who wins when employees must make a choice between the *compensation-driven* pressure to increase internal efficiency or exceeding the expectations of a strategic account (which is not tied to their compensation)?

4. Simplify, Simplify, Simplify

Complexity is a major drain on efficiency, effectiveness, cycle time, flexibility, management, resources, and profits. The market leaders of the future will be those organizations that are easiest to do business with and make everything *incredibly convenient*. In fact, one of the greatest added values a supplier can provide is to greatly simplify current practices, making simplicity a competitive advantage. Our collaborators told us loudly and clearly that simplification must be a major rationale for creating alliances and must govern how the partners work together. The following are areas of focus for integrating simplification into the trust-based organization:

⇒ The alliance's vision and joint objectives must be simply stated, clearly articulated, and widely communicated in a way that creates a common understanding to guide the people at every level who must consistently make it happen.

⇒ Clearly understand up front what Tom Muccio calls the "Holy Grail" issues and make certain that everyone on the team knows the limitations. These are issues in both companies that are very sensitive and not subject to change or negotiation without major *positioning* before any conversation about changing them.

⇒ The first order of business is to outline simple prerequisites or "ground rules" for the collaboration. Be certain team members are able to stay focused on the *common good* by eliminating potential downside concerns, i.e. there will be no layoffs, cost savings will be split 50-50, expenses will be shared equally. Establish guidelines on how decisions will be made, who has final vote, and how conflicts will be resolved. Keep criticism centered on the issues and not the people.

⇒ Establish a written set of "Operating Principles" for the work group, as P & G and Wal-Mart did. Refer to them often, especially during disagreements.

⇒ Initial activities should be simple, small, and focused. Trust will be built much more quickly after a few "small wins". This will give both companies the confidence to then tackle the more complex opportunities and establish a framework for working together. Starting out small at first will actually help accelerate the process down the road.

⇒ Avoid "contracts"—instead, create "Memos of Understanding" or "Project Agreements" or "Principles" to clarify mutual goals. We frequently heard that a few *well-intentioned* lawyers can quickly take the focus off the ultimate objectives and destroy the trust relationship.

Mike Cohn points out that contracts really define the rules for disengaging from a relationship, rather than defining rules to stay engaged. Tom Muccio agrees that contracts are designed to protect against past and potential offenders, and that they can become a real drain on building more trusting relationships.

⇒ Bose substantially sped up the process by setting up *evergreen* contracts that they negotiate once and keep in place. The evergreen contracts include an incentive to reduce costs, with the savings being shared. They have found this is much more effective than the time consuming "bid and re-bid" rituals that eventually put customer and supplier in an adversarial, low trust relationship.

⇒ Set up a simple, but frequent, communications process to keep senior executives informed about alliance "wins", progress, and potential roadblocks. You need them in your corner, so keep them informed about how the alliance is benefiting the company and its customers.

5. Make Technology Your Servant

Technology can be the necessary enabler and accelerator for building trust-based alliances. It is essential when the organizations' customers, suppliers, and business units are widely dispersed geographically, which is the case with the large enterprises that can benefit most by an alliance strategy. On the other hand, technology can be an inhibitor that limits how far you can go. Technology must respond to the needs and objectives of the customer-supplier partnership—not the other way around. Here are some recommendations regarding technology:

⇒ Involve MIS from the beginning as an integral part of the team -- too often, MIS gets involved when it's too late for them to add value. The sooner both organizations' information systems groups become involved, the better. Systems integration issues must be identified and addressed from the start. Determine your long-term objectives first and then design-in the necessary systems support.

⇒ According to S4 Consulting, a networked real-time computer system by which the customer company and all supplier functions can monitor and manage their interaction is deemed to be a critical strategic component. A.T. Kearney observes that leading manufacturers and distributors are rapidly building electronic links with their entire global supply chain, where everyone in the system has access. Leading retailers want suppliers to dramatically improve logistics using EDI.

⇒ Trust is essential when considering granting other companies access to your information systems. The involved organizations must deal with the confidentiality issues that will surface and balance the overall upside potential and the implied risks. The organizations are making themselves *vulnerable*. Each must understand this vulnerability and never use it to their short-term advantage -- to do so would shatter the trust and destroy the relationship.

⇒ When defining the scope of the technology initiatives, be sure to address the communications, measurement, and tracking requirements.

⇒ Bose works through a combination of in-plant partners

and EDI systems for vendors where an in-plant presence is not required. In these cases, "reverse EDI" is used where a supplier can look into the customer's MRP system, from his computer halfway around the world, identify material needed, initiate a purchase order, and ship the required material.

6. Measure Well, Act Fast

In the modern sales process, measurements and data are just as important as selling skills and knowledge. In **Chapter II**, Jane Helsing of QI International states that trust measurement is based on two components: *actual performance* and *subjective feelings*. Customers base the amount of trust they are willing to assign to NAMs and their organizations on these two factors, with actual performance carrying substantially more weight. Actual performance refers to the areas which can be evaluated by finite operational measurements, i.e., on-time delivery, complete order fulfillment, invoice accuracy, quality, etc. Subjective feelings refers to the belief-set which customers formulate regarding a supplier's ability to meet their needs in the future -- this belief is based on emotional evaluation and difficult to measure.

With customers placing increased emphasis on "hard" performance data and less on "softer" relationship oriented experiences, a measurement system which provides real time *actionable* information is imperative. Positive quantifiable results will help build trust and earn more business, and should be communicated frequently and widely. When measurements indicate results are falling short of objectives, the specific problem areas need to be isolated and quickly acted upon to remedy the situation. Intense competition has ended the days where average performance will be tolerated based on the length and depth of the relationship.

Some areas to keep in mind when formulating measurement and action plans are as follows:

⇒ The market, competitors, and, most importantly, customers are continually raising the bar and increasing standards of performance. Continuous improvement has become a business imperative. Suppliers must therefore be internally driven to raise their own performance levels and proactively bring new initiatives to their customers. Trust is built more rapidly when this occurs on a regular basis. However, it is a two-way street, where the customer must be willing to provide the incentive of sharing the upside financial improvement with the supplier.

⇒ A component of high-trust relationships is access to pertinent data flow by customer and supplier. There is extensive sharing of measurement on a real-time basis, which improves efficiency, lets everyone know how he or she is doing, and results in quick action to correct variances. Confidentiality issues around measurements are often the inhibitors or accelerators of progress.

⇒ Set quantitative measures, i.e. "1 to 5", for determining where the relationship stands regarding trust. These can be applied to informal criteria such as: accepted as an insider, expanding spending limits, involvement in strategy, etc. Improvement in informal measurements over time can limit the impact of a mistake of failure, which is discussed in **Chapter II**.

⇒ Proctor & Gamble and Wal-Mart stress the absolute importance in demonstrating *early wins* to build trust and enthusiasm for working toward common goals.

This can not be done without a measurement system in place and defined success criteria.

⇒ The "ability to test" is the best way to resolve differences of opinion. Testing procedures, measurement criteria, and definition of results should be in place.

⇒ Expectations can vary greatly by customer. Find out what four or five areas are most important to top customers. Then, have customers honestly evaluate your performance against these areas. Make it a high priority to close the gap on areas with variance. This will align customer and supplier priorities and enable resources to be focused on areas of highest importance.

7. Unleash the Power of People

Customers repeatedly told us that trust must be earned and backed up by both the NAM and the supplier organization. Initially, the trust is based on past experience and reputation of the organization and transferred to the NAM. Over time, the trust transitions to the individuals most involved with the customer at every level of the organization. Therefore, it is imperative that building and keeping customer trust is a high priority throughout the organization. How many times have we heard the story of a major customer being lost through the inappropriate actions of a *well-intentioned* individual or department that were in direct conflict with the customer's expectations? To reduce the risk of this occurring:

⇒ Ensure that everyone in the internal departments shares a consistent view of each key relationship and their role in supporting that relationship. This is especially true in legal and finance. Make sure to involve people from each of these areas on account teams, so that customer expectations and commitments are understood and communicated.

⇒ Like Chrysler and Bose, view suppliers as critical members of your team -- *an extension of the employee base.* Involving people from suppliers as trusted members of the design and engineering group will result in dramatic increases in quality and innovation.

⇒ Building a *dedicated team* of individuals from both companies to address and solve specific challenges will build trust and is critical to moving toward common goals.

⇒ As P&G and Wal-Mart did, move from having all relationships and activities managed only by the buying and selling functions to *total multifunctional* organizational alignment and involvement.

⇒ It is critical to have the "right" people assigned to customer teams, especially in the beginning. Attitude is very important—seek people who are open and willing to do things differently. People who are *trusted within their own organization* will help ensure the support of their colleagues. Tom Muccio cautions that the *wrong* people will set back trust two to three times faster than it took to build.

⇒ Recognition can fuel the effort. Make heroes in both companies of the individuals who take risks and step out to support new behaviors and new directions. This will result in greater support and involvement throughout each organization.

⇒ Look at the recognition and reward system. Make sure it is not the biggest barrier to success. Change it to be sure that it supports the proper behavior and desired results.

⇒ Be sure that everyone involved truly becomes a *team player*. The best inter-company team members leave their rank and title at the door—everybody is equal with the same objectives.

⇒ Make people the most valuable asset. As we saw in **Chapter XII**, Herb Kelleher, chairman of Southwest Airlines, created trust in the customer by focusing on the company's most valuable resource—its employees. "If you really want to put the customer first, then you have to put the employee first! Only the employee who is *turned on* is going to create a fabulous experience for the customer."

8. Lead With Care

Each of this book's contributors emphasize that building a trust-based organization and making the transition to this *new way of doing business* is not easy and takes the commitment of leaders throughout the company. Successful senior managers will make it clear through their actions that customer trust is never to be compromised and that building and earning trust is the job of every employee. Those who give trust *lip service* by tolerating anything less will have a very difficult journey. The bottom line is that leaders must show they care:

⇒ It is the leader's responsibility to communicate an end-to-end vision and keep the organization focused on the ultimate end-customer.

⇒ Leaders need to always be looking for the win-win. It is important for things to be "fair"—not necessarily equal. A key point brought out in **Chapter VII** is that senior management has to be willing to allow a win-win environment to develop. While many talk about win-win partnerships, their competitive background often makes it difficult to accept the success of the other company when it actually happens.

⇒ We consistently heard that a trust-based organization must involve people with authority. The team leaders on both sides have to deal with many different departments, each with their own agenda, and find a way to speak with *one voice* that speaks with the ultimate consumer in mind.

⇒ Leaders must add the sense of urgency and priority needed to overcome the inertia of their company's traditional practices. P&G and Wal-Mart moved forward only when senior management came to the conclusion that their business process was *very broken*. It is important to start with the "decision" to change. The leaders of both companies actions signal a willingness to invest in the relationship, because the relationship is expected to grow in importance and value over time.

⇒ One of the more difficult things for many senior managers to comprehend and do is to listen to a customer's desires and then modify their processes to meet them. Used to getting their own way, leaders tend to fall into the trap of saying, "Just tell them 'that's our policy'—if they don't like it, they can do business with someone else."

⇒ Leaders of these efforts must constantly keep the group focused on moving the process forward, while looking out for the best interests of all parties. This is not an easy task due to the strong personalities of the people on the alliance teams. The focus must remain continually on meeting established deadlines and moving toward the higher goals of the partnership.

⇒ Tom Peters argues that the true job of the CEO is to get everybody moving in *roughly the same direction*. Doug Bosse believes this is also the true job of leaders and NAMs of suppliers serving strategic accounts.

⇒ *Selling Power* magazine has often carried articles recounting how the most effective leaders build trust by encouraging people to rally behind an idea dedicated to the common good.

So, What's Stopping You—Top 10 Reasons Everybody's Not Doing It

Life teaches that the task is always hardest for the pioneers who must figure out the way, as they blaze new trails. Those who follow in their footsteps have an increasingly easier time. They learn from those who went before them who are willing to share the map, which enables them to proceed more quickly. In the preceding chapters, our collaborators generously shared their maps with the belief that we'll all be far better off when the majority of organizations make building mutually beneficial trust-based alliances a normal practice. Perhaps just as important as learning what to do is understanding the barriers and inevitable road-blocks that can impede your progress. Here are the *top ten reasons* that our contributors say will cause most attempts to build trust-based partnerships between customers and suppliers to fail:

1. *Fear of overdependence.* Many customers harbor a mis-placed fear that they will be held hostage by their suppliers if they allow themselves to become too dependent on them. They believe they are better off keeping suppliers at arms-length and using power (instilling fear that they'll go elsewhere) to get the most favorable terms and results.

2. *Fear of commitment.* In many customer/supplier rela-tionships, *lack of trust* has gone on so long that it has become part of the culture. The end result is both sides being so obsessed with protecting themselves that neither side cares about the other's well being. This transactional relationship keeps ties very nar-row and inhibits any hope of joint venture opportu-nities.

3. *Surprises.* Nothing goes exactly as planned. Don't embarrass your senior management supporters by hiding problems. Communicate potential setbacks early and enlist help in turning around the situation.

4. *Short-term thinking.* Occurs when decisions are made that are detrimental to the relationships. This hap-pens when the individual discipline, department, or business unit objectives are not in line with the mutual objectives agreed upon by both companies.

5.	*Rewards really do work.* This statement became a standing joke with P & G. Often the real culprit in making "short term thinking" prevail is the rewards and recognition programs driving internally focused behavior, which is in conflict with partnership goals. The incentive program must be aligned to drive behavior toward achieving alliance objectives.

6.	*Initiatives without funding.* As recommended in **Chapter VII**, determine the cost *before* actually starting to build the relationship. Tom Muccio's law that "You'll never get a return on investment if you're unwilling to make the investment" certainly applies.

7.	*Contracts can kill.* The very nature of the process, language and terms often wrings the trust out of the relationship. The faith has to be in each other and the opportunity to benefit on a long-term basis.

8.	*Culture encroachment.* This occurs when one party does not understand or respect the other's culture and acts in a way contrary to the culture.

9.	*Loose lips sink partnerships.* Nothing will destroy trust faster than not honoring confidentiality. The most effective partnerships involve mutual access to proprietary information deemed necessary to improve processes. When a company allows an *outside organization* within its confidential circle, it is a strong signal that the potential for the relationship is highly valued. A violation of this trust will be seen as an unforgivable offense.

10. *I'd rather do it myself.* This occurs when the organization truly believes that it possesses an extraordinary degree of competence in all areas of the end-to-end process. It can foster a myopic *not invented here* attitude where new ideas are stifled and the goal becomes perpetuating legacy processes.

That's Our Story and We're Sticking To It!

When Lisa, Mike, and I first began discussing the importance of "trust" in enabling enterprises to move to *new ways of doing business*, we were approaching the subject with strong intuitive feelings that there was something there. When we looked into what research had been done to substantiate this mutual feeling, we kept coming across studies that touched on the subject, but always from a perspective of the importance of "integrity" in the sales and delivery processes.

We began investigating rumors among NAMA members that there was a *new strain of relationships* developing between some very forward-thinking organizations that was leading to results far beyond what people thought possible. We've attempted to provide an overview on the many approaches companies are undertaking, in their own words, from their perspective. These organizations are truly redefining sales, relationships and the traditional way of doing business. When you listen to the people who have been involved in the process for a while, there is no question in your mind that they're onto something big. Let's revisit what two of them said:

"Once this basic and rather substantial act of faith and trust is accomplished, a wide range of daily business activities can be improved beyond today's norms."
Lance Dixon, Executive Director, JIT II Education & Research Center

"Establishing trust between companies is not easy, is often fragile, and requires significant maintenance to sustain; but having lived the benefits for the last ten years, I can't believe there's any better way to do business."
Tom Muccio, VP Customer Business Development, (Wal-Mart), Procter & Gamble

As we looked beyond the sales process to understand every aspect of the business relationship, the role of "trust" became very clear. Trust is not only an essential building block for a strong, growing, mutually beneficial partnership—it is the *keystone*. Once a skilled mason has the keystone in place, his arch becomes a strong bridge, between two points, that can support massive weight. As long as the keystone doesn't shift or crumble, the arch can withstand extraordinary pressure. Yet, remove the keystone and everything falls apart. We believe this metaphor perfectly describes the role of trust—hence, our title, **The Trust Imperative**.

After spending a great deal of time with our book's thought-leaders, we are convinced that there is a *trust imperative*. If you wish to take your organization to new heights, we encourage you to follow in their footsteps. That's our story and we're sticking to it!

APPENDIX

About the Authors:

DOUGLAS A. BOSSE

Douglas A. Bosse is a senior consultant for S4 Consulting. He specializes in facilitating the creation and implementation of relationship management strategies. Doug mentors his clients to systematically monitor, develop and protect their critical relationships. He also provides conflict resolution and mediation guidance to help clients recover their threatened accounts.

Doug has helped numerous clients in a variety of industries to understand the strategic value of their customer relationships; determine future relationship objectives and goals; articulate competitive strengths and weaknesses in meeting the needs of these strategic accounts; and align their organizations to meet new strategic account guidelines.

Doug has overseen many aspects of the primary research phase of relationship management studies, including developing measurement plans, leading qualitative analysis, conducting executive interviews, and developing recommendations for new strategic approaches and improved implementation models. He has also facilitated account teams to develop new strategies and processes.

Doug presented his views on proactive national account planning at the National Account Management Association (NAMA) 1996 Annual Conference. He is currently Vice President of the 1998 Annual Conference at NAMA and serves on the board of directors. In addition, Doug has published numerous articles on strategic account management in S4 Consulting's *The S4 Report*. He has also published articles on management information systems and logistics. Doug serves as the co-director of S4 Consulting's annual international study on innovative practices in strategic account management. This study is conducted in conjunction with NAMA.

Doug received his B.S. from Miami University, and his M.B.A. from The Ohio State University.

JOSEPH P. CANNON

Joseph P. Cannon, Ph.D. is Assistant Professor of Marketing at the College of Business, Colorado State University. Before pursuing an academic career, Professor Cannon worked for six years in technical sales and marketing for the Eastman Kodak Company. He received his BS in Business from Marquette University and his Ph.D. from the University of North Carolina at Chapel Hill and taught at Emery University before moving to Colorado State University in 1997. Joe's research, teaching and consulting activities focus on relationship marketing, business marketing, distribution management, and key account management.

MICHAEL COHN

Mike has 20+ years with HP, including 5 years as a computer systems sales representative, 2 years as a District Sales Manager (focused on the Fortune 100), 10 years as the Global Account Manager (responsible for GE), 2 years as sales planning and quality manager, and the last year as the

Manager of Global Sales Programs for HP Computer Organization.

Mike spoke at NAMA's Leadership Symposium in September of 1997, and wrote a chapter for the new NAMA book on Trust. He has also presented for the Conference Board and various Fortune 100 companies.

At Hewlett-Packard Company he has been honored at the top 300 club, Achievers Club, Account Team of the Year.

LANCE DIXON

Lance Dixon, of Bose Corporation, is the creator of the JIT II concept and management techniques now in practice in many *Fortune 500* companies. Mr. Dixon's career has been in creating and restructuring Purchasing, Transportation, and Distribution organizations. *Business Week* named Bose one of the world-class champs in supplier management while Mr. Dixon was Director of Purchasing at Bose.

JIT II is the subject of case studies by the Harvard Business School and Darden Graduate School and a front-page feature story by the *Wall Street Journal.*

Currently, Bose has been moved to support the national and increasing international adoption of the JIT II concept in the business and academic community, by announcement of the "JIT II Education & Research Center." Bose will operate the Education Center on a non-profit basis donating all revenue in excess of expenses to educational scholarships.

Mr. Dixon is now the Executive Director of the JIT II Education & Research Center.

PATRICIA M. DONEY, Ph.D.

Patricia M. Doney, Ph.D., is Associate Professor of Marketing at the College of Business, Florida Atlantic University. Before pursuing an academic career, Professor Doney worked for nine years in consumer and industrial marketing. She received her MBA from Georgia State University and her Ph.D. from the University of North Carolina at Chapel Hill. Pat's research, teaching and consulting activities focus on international marketing, industrial marketing, and customer satisfaction. This article is based in part on previous research conducted by Professor Doney and Professor Cannon, which is published in the Journal of Marketing.

ROGER J. DOW

Roger Dow is Vice President, General Sales Manager for Marriott: Lodging. As Marriott's lead customer advocate, he works with a 3,000-person sales force for over 1,500 properties worldwide. Starting as a lifeguard at Marriott's sixth hotel, he learned the service business from a "hands-on-perspective." During his 25 years with Marriott, he has directed every aspect of sales and marketing, including: advertising, public relations, promotion, sales training, compensation and succession planning.

Mr. Dow has earned a reputation as one of the most creative and innovative people in the service industry. He developed Marriott's Honored Guest Awards Program, which is ranked as the nation's leading Frequent Traveler Program. Believing that customer and associate retention are the key factors of long-term success, Mr. Dow introduced the Quality Improvement Process at Marriott.

HarperCollins recently published TURNED ON-Eight Vital Insights to Energize Your People, Customers and Profits, which Roger co-authored with Susan Cook. It is a practical hands-on guide on how to inspire people, enthuse customers, and maximize profits.

Roger Dow is Co-Founder of "The Service/Quality Leadership Forum 2000". The members are from America's most respected values driven organizations and are committed to customer satisfaction, quality and team empowerment. The Forum is dedicated to building competitive advantage through service/quality leadership principles and practices.

Roger Dow has worked with the Tom Peters Group as an executive consultant. He is dedicated to helping multi-unit organizations achieve long term differentiation and sustained growth by empowering their associates to understand and exceed customer expectations on a consistent basis. His high-energy presentations are laced with humor and practical "real-world" examples.

The American Society of Association Executives honored Roger as the twelfth industry recipient of their prestigious Academy of Leaders Award. He has served on the board of directors for: the American Society of Association Executives; ASAE Foundation; Hotel Sales and Marketing Association International Foundation; Institute of Certified Travel Agents and National Business Education Association.

Roger Dow has lectured on quality and achieving customer satisfaction at the following business schools: Arizona State University, George Washington University, Rochester Institute of Technology, Texas A&M, University of Southern California, University of South Carolina, Utah State and Tulane.

From 1969 to 1971 he served in the United States Army with the 101st Airborne Division in Vietnam where he received the Bronze Star and other citations. In 1968, Mr. Dow received his B.S. in psychology from Seton Hall University, where he was senior class president, captain of the varsity wrestling team and secretary of Tau Kappa Epsilon Fraternity. He was named TKE alumnus of the year for 1991 and was presented with the award by President Ronald Reagan.

Roger resides in Bethesda, Maryland with his wife and two children.

GERHARD GSCHWANDTNER

Gerhard Gschwandtner is the founder and publisher of SELLING POWER, a national magazine designed to help companies increase their sales success. After eight years in international sales and training for a French construction equipment manufacturer, he started a sales training consulting company in 1977. He trained over 10,000 salespeople in the United States and Europe.

In 1981 Gschwandtner created a newspaper tabloid for sales managers with the objective to sell his sales training services. The first publication was so successful that sales managers purchased thousands of extra copies for distribution to their sales staff. Without the help from outside investors, and relying on a shoestring budget he developed the publication into the nation's leading sales magazine with a circulation of 250,000. Today, the magazine has subscribers in 67 countries worldwide.

Gerhard is the author of eleven books on the subject of selling and motivation. (Superachievers, Supersellers, The Sales Questions Book, Nonverbal Selling Power, The Sales

Manager's Problem Solver, How to Become a Master Sales Builder, Selling Power's Best, Thoughts to Sell By, The Sales Closing Book and The Psychology of Sales Success).

He is the recipient of Sales and Marketing Management's Award for Excellence in sales training. In 1996, Selling Power received Folio Magazine's prestigious award for editorial excellence. In 1997 Selling Power was honored with the "Outstanding Publication of the Year" award by the National Society of Business Press Editors. In 1997 Gerhard launched Selling Power Live! It is an audio magazine that reaches over 10,000 sales executives nationwide. In 1998 he created an interactive video sales-training program entitled Nonverbal Selling Power, the first course to teach nonverbal communication techniques together with professional selling skills.

Gerhard has a degree in business administration from Salzburg, Austria and has conducted post-graduate studies at the Sorbonne in Paris, France. He is fluent in German, French and English. In his spare time he loves sailing, skiing, kayaking, Ping-Pong and golfing. Gerhard's wife is the editor of the magazine and the author of two children's books. The Gschwandtner's have three daughters and live in Fredericksburg, VA.

JANE HELSING

Jane Helsing is Vice President of Strategic Accounts for QI International, Inc. a consulting firm that offers an innovative yet common-sense approach to customer relationship management. QI International's corporate office is located in St. Paul, Minnesota with affiliate offices located throughout the United States, in Europe, Asia, and South Africa.

Ms. Helsing works with a variety of Fortunes 500 companies to help them focus on creating committed customers. Her consulting work includes tailoring tools that will help employees manage and assess the quality of relationships with their customers, suppliers and work teams, as well as ensuring the leaders of these organizations are able to incorporate findings into longer-range planning efforts. The tools that Ms. Helsing introduces to her customers cover areas such as feedback, measurement, data information interpretation, and planning. She also provides direction to a team of QI International consultants who manage their own portfolios of work.

Ms. Helsing spent 16 years in the telecommunications industry, where for several years she directed one of the business unit's forecasting and market/competitive analysis functions. She consulted with senior managers regarding the implications of marketplace changes and developed new approaches to analyzing and forecasting in a rapidly changing industry. She is also experienced in the management of large field teams, having managed a 450-person customer service organization.

Ms. Helsing is currently the President of the National Account Management Association (NAMA). She has held that position since 1997. Since 1996 to the present, Ms. Helsing has been a member of NAMA's Board of Directors.

Ms. Helsing received her masters degree in Statistics in 1980 from Rutgers University. She received her bachelor of arts degree in Mathematics with an emphasis in Computer Science at Susquehanna University in 1976.

GARY M. KUNATH

Gary M. Kunath had the responsibility for the sales, management and quality training for AT&T worldwide. He was instrumental in building the skills/competency model for "World Class" sales performance within AT&T and the supporting training curriculum. He consults and supports businesses in their initiatives to transform managers into leaders and coaches to enhance the development of their people and in re-encultering their sales force taking them to the next level of performance. He specializes in helping Fortune 1000 companies gain a sustainable competitive advantage through achieving salesforce and management / leadership superiority.

He is founder of The Summit Group, a firm that specializes in providing customized training and consulting services in the areas of Leadership, Sales/Marketing Skills, and Management Development. The Summit Group offers customized training programs on business value selling, strategic thinking for sales teams, effective presentation skills, transforming sales people into business people, account management using the internet, relationship development & management, value generation and offer development, executive selling, and leading re-engineered employees, and building business alliances and partnerships.

The Summit Groups' client list includes such companies as Marriott International, AT&T, Perstorp Flooring, Mannington Carpets, 3M, Fisher Scientific, Group W Communications, SBC Communications, Savannah Foods & Industries, RR Donnelley & Sons, Schlumberger, Southern California Edison, IKNO, Lubrizol, BellSouth, CBIS, Boise Cascade, and Delta Air Lines to name a few. Mr. Kunath was a certified Malcolm Baldrige National Quality Examiner and sat on AT&T's Chairman's Quality Award Board of Examiners. He was part of the effort that resulted in AT&T winning three National Malcolm Baldrige Quality Awards in 1992 and 1994.

He regularly lectures in the Executive Education and MBA Programs of Duke University's Fuqua School of Business, Emory University Business School and at Cornell University's Johnson Graduate School of Management. He is a requested speaker by such organizations as National Account Management Association (NAMA), Cable Television Administration and Marketing Association (CTAM), International Management Council, Women in Cable and Telecommunications, Penn State University's' Annual Cable Television Conference, Clemson University's Organization Excellence Conference and has recently been appointed to the Board of Directors of NAMA as VP of Education. He is a contributing author of "Unlocking Profits". His company was featured in *Selling Power* magazine (Sept. 1997) as one of the top training companies in the country in the areas of value generation, offer development, relationship management, developing business acumen, proactive innovation and knowledge acquisition using the Internet.

Mr. Kunath was a National Account Manager with AT&T's Business Markets Group where he earned 13 consecutive Sales Vice President Awards for top sales in the country and won three consecutive National Leaders Council Awards given annually to individuals whose team sales results rank in the top 2% in the country. Mr. Kunath holds an MS degree in Organizational Development from the State University of New York at Binghamton, a BS degree in Business Administration from Syracuse University and an AAS in Business Management from Mohawk Valley Community College. He is also an August 1990 graduate of Duke University's Executive Development Program.

JORDAN D. LEWIS

Jordan Lewis, an expert on business alliances, is often called a "corporate marriage counselor." Companies worldwide seek his help to build best alliance performance from the start or to repair weak alliances. He typically works with both firms involved in an alliance.

He is the author of *The Connected Corporation* (1995) and *Partnerships for Profit* (1990), both published by Simon and Schuster/Free Press. *Business Week's* review of his latest book said: "This readable book provides a realistic road map for forging true alliances." The *Wall Street Journal* said it "meticulously dissects customer-supplier alliances to reveal what makes the best ones tick." The Financial Times called Partnerships "extremely useful. .a thinking manager's guide to alliances." Together, these books have been published in 12 languages. His next book on alliances will be published by Harvard Business School Press.

Lewis's work has been featured in *The Wall Street Journal, The Economist, The Financial Times, The Japan Times, Modern Healthcare, New Civil Engineer,* and other publications. His Op-Ed pieces on alliances have appeared in *The Wall Street Journal* and *The New York Times;* he also has been a guest on CNN, National Public Radio and Reuters TV. A popular speaker, Lewis has addressed major audiences for *Business Week, The Economist, Fortune,* The Strategic Leadership Forum, Management Centre Europe, Keidanren (Tokyo), Singapore Institute of Management and the World Economic Forum, among others. Based in Switzerland, the World Economic Forum (an organization that brings together global leaders to discuss major current issues) named him a Fellow in recognition of his contributions.

TOM A. MUCCIO

Tom Muccio is Vice President of Customer Business Development (Wal-Mart), Procter & Gamble Worldwide. He is a member of NAMA and serves on its Board of Directors.

Muccio has been with P&G for 27 years in a variety of sales and marketing assignments in both the United States and abroad, including the position of national sales manager. He was part of the pioneering group that invented the multi-functional customer team concept at P&G, and he has been the team leader since the inception of the highly successful and much-publicized Wal-Mart / P&G relationship.

Beginning in 1994, Muccio was made responsible for the expansion of the customer business development concept to other P&G countries worldwide, as well as extending the Wal-Mart / P&G relationship on a global basis.

Mr. Muccio spends his spare time working in a leadership position with a variety of Christian ministries. Also, he is on the advisory board at both Ohio University College of Business and the American Studies Institute at Harding University.

LISA NAPOLITANO

Ms. Napolitano joined the National Account Management Association in 1991 as Executive Director charged with revitalizing the professional association founded in 1964. Her primary responsibility is to create new educational opportunities and informational deliverables for the NAMA membership and the business community at large. Ms. Napolitano is also charged with directing the marketing, promotion, and membership development for the association.

Ms. Napolitano serves as chief spokesperson for the organization, seeking out opportunities to increase awareness of both NAMA and the concepts of strategic customer-supplier partnering.

During her tenure, Ms. Napolitano has developed numerous strategic alliances with like-minded organizations in the media, academic, and corporate arenas. Under her direction, NAMA has grown tenfold and now boasts a range of leading-edge information including numerous research and benchmarking projects, a fully interactive website, a quarterly journal, and a proprietary resource library.

Ms. Napolitano currently serves on the Board of Directors of the National Account Management Association, The Center for Professional Selling at Baylor University, and the Center for Consultative Selling at Ohio University. She served as co-editor and contributing author of *Unlocking Profits: The Strategic Advantage of Key Account Management*, which was independently published by NAMA in the spring of 1997.

Prior to joining NAMA, Ms. Napolitano was in retail management and buying at both Macys and Bloomingdales in New York City. She received her Bachelor of Arts Degree in Politics from Princeton University in 1989. She currently resides in the city of Chicago where NAMA is headquartered.

JOHN L. NEUMAN

Mr. Neuman is a Vice President with A. T. Kearney and is a member of the firm's Operations/Supply Chain Practice.

Areas of expertise:
Supply Chain Management and Partnering
Manufacturing Strategy
Visioning through to Implementation
"Voice of the Customer" and Market Assessments
Competitive Assessments and Benchmarking
Organization Structures and Transformations
Overhead Value Analysis
Change Management/Leadership
Total Quality and Team-Based Organization cultures

Prior work experience
John has over 27 years of consulting experience in North America, Europe and the Far East. In recent years, his work has focused particularly on strategy and marketing as they couple to supply chain and business process opportunities to enhance customer/consumer satisfaction.

He has worked extensively in industrial, consumer goods and service-based companies, including packaged goods, pharmaceuticals, chemicals, automotive, utilities and electronics, financial services, and medical products.

Speeches and Articles
Mr. Neuman speaks frequently at industry forums, lectures at several leading graduate business schools, and his articles have appeared in Harvard Business Review, Management Review, Marketing News, Journal of Business Strategy, and Supply Chain Management.

Education
BEE in Electrical Engineering, Cornell University
Masters in Engineering, Cornell University
MBA in Industrial Management/Management Science, University of Pennsylvania

MICHAEL A. PUSATERI

Michael Pusateri is Vice President of Interactive Sales and Marketing for Marriott International. His responsibilities include Marriott International's internet and intranet strategies as well as Marriott's' consumer website. He is also responsible for alliance activities with technology marketing companies and global distribution systems.

Prior to his most recent appointment, Pusateri served as Vice President of Business Travel Sales for Marriott International. In this capacity he was responsible for managing Marriott Lodgings' large account sales force.

Before joining Marriott in 1990 he held a variety of sales and marketing positions of increasing responsibility at Holiday Corporation, where he managed multi-brand partner strategies on behalf of Embassy Suites, Hampton Inns, Harrahs Casino's and the Holiday Inn brand. He also was responsible for airline and hotel marketing at Avis Rent a Car.

Pusateri is a graduate of the University of Connecticut where he earned a bachelor of science degree in marketing.

In addition, he teaches the Basics of Hotel Sales at Cornell University and E-commerce in the MBA program at the University of Maryland.

Mike is President, Emeritus of the National Account Management Association. He also holds a seat on the board of the directors of Marriott's Federal Credit Union,

Hospitality Sales and Marketing Association International and the Association of Travel Marketing Executives.
He is also co-author of *Unlocking Profits: The Strategic Advantage of Key Account Management.*

LARRY R. SMELTZER

Larry Smeltzer is a Professor of Supply Chain Management at Arizona State University where he teaches and conducts research on purchasing management. His research has lead to a number of articles in such journals as the European Journal of Purchasing, the International Journal of Purchasing and Supply Management, Harvard Business Review and Sloan Management Review. He is also the director of two annual seminars at Arizona State University and has worked with a large number of organizations on various aspects of Purchasing Management. He has conducted seminars and worked with organizations in Asia, Europe, Mexico and throughout the U.S.

ADDITIONAL RESOURCES

Athos, Anthony G., and John I. Gabarro, *Interpersonal Behavior, Communication, and Understanding in Relationships*, Prentice-Hall, (1978).

Barber, Bernard, *The Logic and Limits of Trust*, Rutgers University Press, (1983).

Bromiley, P., & L. L. Cummings, *Organizations with Trust: Theory and Measurement*, Working paper, University of Minnesota, (August, 1993). Also presented at the 53rd annual meeting of the Academy of Management, Atlanta, GA.

Butler, J., "Toward Understanding and Measuring Conditions of Trust: Evolution of a Conditions of Trust Inventory", *Journal of Management*, vol. 17(3), (1991), pp. 643-663.

Burt, D. N., and M.F. Doyle, *The American Keiretsu: A Strategic Weapon for Global Competitiveness*, Business One Irwin, (1993).

Cannon, Joseph P., Gregory T. Gundlach and Narakesari Narayandas, *Issues of Trust in Customer-Supplier Partnering*, (April 28, 1997).

Dasgupta, Partha, *Trust as a Commodity, in Trust: Making and Breaking Cooperative Relations*, Diego Gambetta, ed., New York: Basil Blackwell, Inc.

Doney, Patricia M. and Joseph P. Cannon, "An Examination of the Nature of Trust in Buyer-Seller Relationships", *Journal of Marketing*, vol. 61, (April 1997), pp. 35-51.

Dwyer, F. Robert and Rosemary R. Legace, "On the Nature and Role of Buyer-Seller Trust", *In AMA Summer Edcator's Conference Proceedings*, Series 52, eds. T. Shimpt et al., (1986), pp. 40-45. Chicago: American Marketing Association.

Ellram, L.M.," Partnering Pitfalls and Success Factors", *International Journal of Purchasing and Materials Management*, vol. 31 (2), (Spring 1995), pp. 36-44.

Fisher, Roger, and Scott Brown, *Getting Together: Building Relationships as We Negotiate*, Penguin Books, (1989).

Frost, Taggart F. and Farzad Moussavi, "The Relationship Between Leader Power Base and Influence: The Moderating Role of Trust", *Journal of Applied Business Research*, vol. 8 (4), (1992), pp. 9-14.

Gabarro, J., *The Dynamics of Taking Charge*, Boston: Harvard Business School Press, (1987).

Gambetta, D., Can we trust trust? In D. Gambetta (Ed.), *Trust: Making and Breaking Cooperative Relations*, pp. 213-237, Oxford, UK: Basil Blackwell, (1988).

Ganesan, Shankar, " Determinants of Long-Term Orientation in Buyer-Seller Relationships", *Journal of Marketing*, vol. 58, (April), pp. 1-19.

Handy, Charles, "Trust and the Virtual Organization", *Harvard Business Review*, (May-June 1995).

Hawes, Jon M., Kenneth E. Mast and John E. Swan, "Trust Earning Perceptions of Sellers and Buyers", *Journal of Personal Selling & Sales Management*, vol. 9, (Spring 1989), pp. 1-8.

Heide, Jan B. and George John, "Alliances in Industrial Purchasing: The Determinants of Joint Action in Buyer-Supplier Relations", *Journal of Marketing Research*, vol. 27, (February 1990), pp. 24-36.

Hendrick T. and L.M. Ellram, *Strategic Supplier Partnerships: An International Study*, Center for Advanced Purchasing Studies, (1993).

Hosmer, L.T., "Trust: The Connecting Link Between Organizational Theory and Philosophical Ethics", *Academy of Management Review*, vol. 20, no. 2, (April 1995), pp. 379-403.

Johnston, Wesley J. and Jeffrey E. Lewin, "Organizational Buying Behavior: Toward an Integrative Framework", *Journal of Business Research*, vol. 35, (1996), pp. 1-15.

Kanter, R., *When Giants Learn to Dance*. New York: Simon & Schuster, (1989).

Katzenbach, J.R. & D. K. Smith, *The Wisdom of Teams: Creating the High-Performance Organization*. Boston: Harvard Business School Press, (1993).

Kirkpatrick, S., & E. Locke, "Leadership: Do Traits Matter?" *Academy of Management Executive*, vol. 5(2), (1991), pp. 48-60.

Kumar, Nirmalya," The Power of Trust in Manufacturer-Retailer Relationships", *Harvard Business Review*, (November-December 1996).

Landeros, R. and R.M. Monczka, "Cooperative Buyer-Seller Relationships and a Firm's Competitive Posture", *Journal of Purchasing and Materials Management*, vol. 25(3), (1989), pp. 9-18.

Lewis, Jordan D., *Partnerships For Profit: Structuring and Managing Strategic Alliances*, Free Press, (1990).

Lewis, Jordan D., *The Connected Corporation*, Free Press, (1995).

Lorenz, E. H., "Trust and the Flexible Firm", *Industrial Relations*, vol. 31(3), (1992), pp. 455-472.

McCauley, Dan P. and Karl W. Kuhnert, "A Theoretical Review and Empirical Investigation of Employee Trust in Management", *Public Administration Quarterly*, (Summer 1992), pp. 265-84.

Michalos, Alex C., "The Impact of Trust on Business, International Security and the Quality of Life", *Journal of Business Ethics*, vol. 9, (1990), pp. 619-638.

Milliman, Ronald E. and Douglas Fugate, "Using Trust Transference as a Persuasion Technique: An Empirical Field Investigation", *Journal of Personal Selling and Sales Management*, vol. 8, (August 1988), pp. 1-7.

Moorman, Christine, Rohit Deshpande and Gerald Zaltman, "Factors Affecting Trust in Market Research Relationships", *Journal of Marketing*, vol. 57, (January 1993), pp. 31-101.

Morgan, Robert M. and Shelby D. Hunt, "The Commitment-Trust Theory of Relationship Marketing", *Journal of Marketing*, vol. 58, (July 1994), pp. 20-38.

Pauchant, T.C., & I. I. Mitroff, *Transforming the Crisis-Prone Organization: Preventing Individual, Organizational, and Environmental Tragedies.* San Francisco: Jossey-Bass, (1992).

Sako, M., *Prices, Quality, and Trust: Inter-Firm Relations in Britain & Japan.* New York: Cambridge University Press, (1992).

Salmond, Deborah, *Refining the Concept of Trust in Business-to-Business Relationship Theory, Research & Management,* University of Baltimore.

Schurr, Paul H. and Julie L. Ozanne, "Influences on Exchange Processes: Buyers' Preconceptions of a Seller's Trustworthiness and Bargaining Toughness", *Journal of Consumer Research*, vol. 11 (4), (March 1985), pp. 939-53.

Scheuing, E., *The Power of Strategic Partnering*, Productivity Press, (1994).

Schmitz, Judith M., Robert Frankel and David J. Frayer, *Efficient Consumer Response Alliances: A Best Practices Model,* Grocery Manufacturers of America, (1995).

Sheridan, John H., "An Alliance Built On Trust", *Industryweek*, (March 17, 1997).

Smeltzer, Larry R.," The Meaning and Origin of Trust in Buyer-Supplier Relationships", *International Journal of Purchasing and Materials Management,* (Winter 1997).

Smith, J. Brock and Donald W. Barclay, *Promoting Effective Selling Alliances: The Roles of Trust and Organizational Differences*, Technical Working Paper, Report no. 95-100, (January 1995).

Sullivan, Jeremiah, Richard B. Peterson, Naoki Kameda, and Justin Shimada, "The Relationship Between Conflict Resolution Approaches and Trust - A Cross Cultural Study", *Academy of Management Journal*, vol. 24 (4), (1981), pp. 803-815.

Swan, John E. and Johannah Jones Nolan, "Gaining Customer Trust: A Conceptual Guide for the Salesperson", *Journal of Personal Selling & Sales Management*, vol. 5 (2), (November 1985), pp. 39-48.

Swan, John E., Fred Trawick, Jr., David R. Rink and Jenny J. Roberts, "Measuring Dimensions of Purchaser Trust of Industrial Salespeople", *Journal of Personal Selling and Sales Management*, vol. 8 (1), (1988), pp. 1-9.

"The Ultimate in Closeness", *Purchasing Magazine*, (April 1997).

Trawick, I. Fred, Jr., and David W. Silva, "How Industrial Salespeople Gain Customer Trust", *Industrial Marketing Management*, vol. 14, (August 1985), pp. 203-11.

Whitney, John O., *The Trust Factor: Liberating Profits and Restoring Corporate Vitality*, McGraw-Hill, Inc., (1994).

Young, Louise C. and Ian F. Wilkinson, "The Role of Trust and Co-operation in Marketing Channels: A Preliminary Study", *European Journal of Marketing*, vol. 23 (2), (1989), pp. 109-22.

Zand, Dale E., "Trust and Managerial Problem Solving", *Administrative Science Quarterly*, vol. 17, (1972), pp. 229-39.

ABOUT THE BOOK SPONSOR: NAMA

NAMA Mission Statement

The National Account Management Association is a non-profit organization devoted to promoting and developing the partnering concepts of national, global, key, corporate and strategic account management. NAMA is dedicated to the professional and personal development of the sales and marketing executives charged with managing such accounts, and to elevating the status of the profession as a whole.

A Brief History

➤ NAMA was founded in 1964 by E. Brooke Lee and a group of sales executives in the chemical industry to respond to a need for training on the specifics of managing large, complex, multi-location accounts.

➤ NAMA services and values apply to all industries. Among our membership are companies in: communications, hospitality, manufacturing, chemicals, electronics, food, paper, health care, textiles, services, utilities, and many other manufacturing segments.

➤ Today, over 1200 members strong, NAMA remains unique in its focus on assisting its members in building and managing successful partnerships with their core accounts.

Benefits & Services

▼ Educational Meetings & Training

- Annual Conference
- Annual Leadership Symposium
- Corporate On-Site Case Studies
- One & Two-Day Seminars

▼ Publications

- Quarterly NAMA Journal
- "Unlocking Profits: The Strategic Advantage of Key Account Management"
- Guidebook of Major Account Management Practices
- Case Study Best Practice Series
- White Paper Library
- Buzz Reports

▼ Surveys & Studies

- Annual Compensation Survey of NAMs & Managers
- Global Account Management Practice
- NAMA / H.R. Chally Benchmarking Consortium
- Strategic Account Management Innovation Study
- Research Report Series

▼ Peer Networking

- Peer "Subject Expert" Directory
- Website-driven Special Interest Groups
- On-line searchable member database
- Career Exchange

The Future

➤ Adoption of national/global account programs by national and international corporations is on the rise. The continuous process of companies reducing their supplier bases requires that firms take measures to become the "preferred supplier" to a core set of customers in order to survive. Having a national / global account strategy is fast becoming the cornerstone of a successful sales organization.

➤ NAMA Membership has grown by 50% in the last year. We predict that by the year 2000, NAMA will be 2000 members strong.

➤ Through the use of sophisticated technology, NAMA has begun to market its products and services worldwide through the Internet, among other venues. Our long-term strategy is to develop satellite chapters of NAMA in key markets across the globe.